DURCAN

CW00541583

80 at 80

Paul Durcan

80 poems by Paul Durcan published on the occasion of his eightieth birthday, 16 October 2024

Edited by Niall MacMonagle
Introduced by Colm Tóibín

Harvill
Secker

1 3 5 7 9 10 8 6 4 2

Harvill Secker, an imprint of Vintage, is part of the Penguin
Random House group of companies whose addresses can be
found at global.penguinrandomhouse.com

Penguin
Random House
UK

First published by Harvill Secker in 2024

penguin.co.uk/vintage

Typeset in 11/14pt Minion Pro by Jouve (UK), Milton Keynes
Printed and bound in Great Britain by Clays Ltd, Elcograf S.p.A.

The authorised representative in the EEA is Penguin Random House Ireland,
Morrison Chambers, 32 Nassau Street, Dublin D02 YH68

A CIP catalogue record for this book is available from the British Library

ISBN 9781787304840

Contents

Introduction

Paul Durcan 80

Paul Durcan's voice as he read from his work and spoke about poetry could be both deadpan and dead serious; it could also be wildly comic and brilliantly indignant.

I loved the undercurrent of anarchy playing against moral seriousness and I began to go to his readings. These were extraordinary performances where many parts were acted out, and where the comedy was undermined by anger sometimes, or pure melancholy, or raw quirkiness, or a sympathy for pain or loss or loneliness.

And, slowly, I began to appreciate the artistry in his poems, the craft, the command.

His poems are open forms filled by voices, often the voice of the poet himself or someone like him, or the voice of a persona he has created or a character he has made. Some of the narrative is shot through with surprise or delight or wonder at the strangeness of the world or the sheer sadness of things. At the centre of Durcan's poetic enterprise is an urge to destabilise and make us re-see what is odd and what is ordinary.

These are both poems of passionate statement and poems that eschew earnestness or easy feeling. While they play in the space between the real and the surreal, they blur these categories. The poet emerges, as though from a lair or a cave, to check out the world, armed with a glittering mind and a moral sense lightened by a delight in misrule, comic timing and tonal grace.

Just as James Joyce in *Ulysses* loved what was playful and parodic, relishing lists and shifts in style, Durcan's imagination is ready for surprise, for an unexpected moment of pure pathos followed by a line or an image that is peculiar or sharply funny. In *Ulysses*, Joyce placed Leopold Bloom's rich consciousness and unusual ways of noticing against a sensibility that was vulnerable. Like Bloom, Durcan can look inwards but often seems most comfortable watching the city, the street, the society around him. Durcan's narrators take delight in what happens. Even his indignation has a streak of dark delight.

But the poems can also be daring, directly personal as well as directly political. It is hard to think of another poet in these islands who has written such searing poems against violence and cruelty and the politics of hate. It is also difficult to think of another male poet who has written such brave works of self-examination. In his poems about his father, for example, or his marriage, or his solitude, Paul Durcan manages a desolation mixed with a fierce generosity of spirit, a hard-won sense of healing edged and tempered by an equally hard-won sense of loss and despondency.

Durcan's public poems are risk-taking explorations of the intersection where tragedy and comedy meet in contemporary Ireland. He can put an antic disposition on, for example, to explode the power of the Catholic Church in a poem such as 'Cardinal Dies of Heart Attack in Dublin Brothel'. In 'The Divorce Referendum, Ireland, 1986', on the other hand, his indignation at a sermon in a church is more unequivocal.

But Durcan's dispute with the Church and religion is essentially one that he also has with himself. The poems come from tensions in his own sensibility. He is torn between what is visible and material and what is numinous and strange. If he seeks transcendence, he wishes his deliverance to come from a place that is rooted and can be named.

Sometimes, Durcan gets enough energy and delight from the ordinary universe that he does not need to soar or reach towards easy grandeur. He is as wary of invoking pure, unmediated nature in a poem as he is of easily made phrases or fine-sounding images. Since there is a river in ' "Windfall", 8 Parnell Hill, Cork', then there will also be, as viewed from a window, 'factory chimneys, / The electricity power station and the car assembly works, / The fleets of trawlers and the pilot tugs', and only then does he write: 'The river a reflection of itself in its own waters.'

Sometimes also, in yoking two unlikely images together, Durcan can create an image of astonishing originality, as in the opening three lines of the second stanza of his poem 'The Pietà's Over':

'The Pietà's over – it is Easter over all our lives:

The revelation of our broken marriage, and its resurrection;

The breaking open of the tomb, and the setting free.'

Durcan knows how to create an arresting opening for a poem, such as the first two lines of 'Raymond of the Rooftops': 'The morning after the night / The roof flew off the house', or the moment at the opening of 'Father's Day, 21 June 1992' when it is clear that the narrator will have to travel with an axe – 'all four-and-a-half feet of it' – on a train to Cork. But both of these poems then become melancholy, thoughtful, almost reticent, while holding on to the initial tone of mayhem and mischief. We watch Durcan as conjuror, capable of handling opposing tone with masterful and disquieting ease.

The poems have a casual, throwaway air. If Durcan is tempted to offer the end of a line a consoling soft sound, he will stop himself. If a poem is taking on the form of a ballad, he will cut back on easy transitions. He likes the untidy mind; he enjoys creating characters who are easily distracted and observe them talking or musing or watching. And then he focuses the poem with an unexpected turn in the diction or in the perception. He gives us a line of pure surprise.

Durcan has little interest in what is ridiculous. Broad comedy doesn't interest him just as he avoids earnestness and solemnity. Rather, he favours what is desperately funny, or what might seem so. 'Tullynoe: Tête-à-Tête in the Parish Priest's Parlour', one of his masterpieces, may be a poem about modernity arriving in a village, but more than that it is a great and grave comic poem.

'Six Nuns Die in Convent Inferno', another of Durcan's masterpieces, is, ostensibly, a poem of lament but it is also a celebration of the peculiarity of nunhood itself, its joys and strangenesses. Durcan lets the voice of the nun-narrator soar, lift up into the heavens, come back down to earth in Dublin, in Stephen's Green, land in a place of ordinary speech – 'But I was no daw. / I knew what a weird bird I was' – with many diversions along the way:

'If you will remember us – six nuns burnt to death –

Remember us for the frisky girls that we were,

Now more than ever kittens in the sun.'

Just as Durcan can explore celibacy and bemoan solitude, he is a rare male contemporary poet who can write easily and naturally about his own heterosexuality. He is, as the title of one of his books suggests, 'crazy about women'. He writes passionate love poems to his wife even after their marriage has ended.

Durcan, in general, is suspicious of what is perfect and complete. But if there is one poem in this book that approaches those conditions, it is a short poem – five four-line stanzas – from his 1978 volume 'Sam's Cross'. The poem is called 'Making Love Outside Áras an Uachtaráin'. (Áras an Uachtaráin, the house of the President of Ireland, was inhabited from 1959 to 1973 by Éamon de Valera whose severe and austere political persona would not have endeared himself to the young poet.)

The poem begins effortlessly, the tone is casual, the line breaks natural. Durcan, it appears, has taken to heart what W. B. Yeats said: 'Above all it is necessary that the lyric poet's life be known, that we should understand that his poetry is no rootless flower but the speech of a man.' Underneath the gravity of the poem's speech, there is someone ready to burst with laughter. Underneath the laughter is a strange seriousness. Beside the wildness, there is tenderness. And these are the tensions that nourish Durcan's imagination and give his poems their powerful and unsettling sound, that are here now distilled and given form.

Colm Tóibín, 2024

O Westport in the Light of
Asia Minor (1975)

Nessa

I met her on the First of August
In the Shangri-La Hotel,
She took me by the index finger
And dropped me in her well.
And that was a whirlpool, that was a whirlpool,
And I very nearly drowned.

Take off your pants, she said to me,
And I very nearly didn't;
Would you care to swim? she said to me,
And I hopped into the Irish Sea.
And that was a whirlpool, that was a whirlpool,
And I very nearly drowned.

On the way back I fell in the field
And she fell down beside me,
I'd have lain in the grass with her all my life
With Nessa:
She was a whirlpool, she was a whirlpool,
And I very nearly drowned.

O Nessa my dear, Nessa my dear,
Will you stay with me on the rocks?
Will you come for me into the Irish Sea
And for me let your red hair down?
And then we will ride into Dublin City
In a taxi-cab wrapped up in dust.
Oh you are a whirlpool, you are a whirlpool,
And I am very nearly drowned.

Ireland 1972

Next to the fresh grave of my belovèd grandmother
The grave of my first love murdered by my brother.

The Girl with the Keys to Pearse's Cottage

to John and Judith Meagher

When I was sixteen I met a dark girl;
Her dark hair was darker because her smile was so bright;
She was the girl with the keys to Pearse's Cottage;
And her name was Cáit Killann.

The cottage was built into the side of a hill;
I recall two windows and a cosmic peace
Of bare brown rooms and on whitewashed walls
Photographs of the passionate and pale Pearse.

I recall wet thatch and peeling jambs
And how all was best seen from below in the field;
I used to sit in the rushes with ledger-book and pencil
Compiling poems of passion for Cáit Killann.

Often she used linger on the sill of a window;
Hands by her side and brown legs akimbo;
In sun-red skirt and moon-black blazer;
Looking toward our strange world wide-eyed.

Our world was strange because it had no future;
She was America-bound at summer's end.
She had no choice but to leave her home –
The girl with the keys to Pearse's Cottage.

O Cáit Killann, O Cáit Killann,
You have gone with your keys from your own native place.
Yet here in this dark – El Greco eyes blaze back
From your Connemara postman's daughter's proudly mortal face.

Teresa's Bar (1976)

The Difficulty that is Marriage

We disagree to disagree, we divide, we differ;
Yet each night as I lie in bed beside you
And you are faraway curled up in sleep
I array the moonlit ceiling with a mosaic of question marks;
How was it I was so lucky to have ever met you?
I am no brave pagan proud of my mortality
Yet gladly on this changeling earth I should live for ever
If it were with you, my sleeping friend.
I have my troubles and I shall always have them
But I should rather live with you for ever
Than exchange my troubles for a changeless kingdom.
But I do not put you on a pedestal or throne;
You must have your faults but I do not see them.
If it were with you, I should live for ever.

Wife Who Smashed Television Gets Jail

'She came home, my Lord, and smashed in the television;
Me and the kids were peaceably watching *Kojak*
When she marched into the living room and declared
That if I didn't turn off the television immediately
She'd put her boot through the screen;
I didn't turn it off, so instead she turned it off –
I remember the moment exactly because Kojak
After shooting a dame with the same name as my wife
Snarled at the corpse – Goodnight, Queen Maeve –
And then she took off her boots and smashed in the television;
I had to bring the kids round to my mother's place;
We got there just before the finish of *Kojak*;
(My mother has a fondness for *Kojak*, my Lord);
When I returned home my wife had deposited
What was left of the television into the dustbin,
Saying – I didn't get married to a television
And I don't see why my kids or anybody else's kids
Should have a television for a father or mother,
We'd be much better off all down in the pub talking
Or playing bar-billiards –
Whereupon she disappeared off back down again to the pub.'
Justice O'Brádaigh said wives who preferred bar-billiards to family
    television
Were a threat to the family which was the basic unit of society
As indeed the television itself could be said to be a basic unit of
    the family
And when as in this case wives expressed their preference in forms
    of violence
Jail was the only place for them. Leave to appeal was refused.

In Memory of those Murdered in the Dublin Massacre, May 1974

In the grime-ridden sunlight in the downtown Wimpy bar
I think of all the crucial aeons – and of the labels
That freedom fighters stick onto the lost destinies of unborn
    children;
The early morning sunlight carries in the whole street from
    outside;
The whole wide street from outside through the plate-glass
    windows;
Wholly, sparklingly, surgingly, carried in from outside;
And the waitresses cannot help but be happy and gay
As they swipe at the tabletops with their dishcloths –
Such a moment as would provide the heroic freedom fighter
With his perfect meat.
And I think of those heroes – heroes? – heroes.

And as I stand up to walk out –
The aproned old woman who's been sweeping the floor
Has mop stuck in bucket, leaning on it;
And she's trembling all over, like a flower in the breeze.
She'd make a mighty fine explosion now, if you were to blow
    her up;
An explosion of petals, of aeons, and the waitresses too, flying
    breasts and limbs,
For a free Ireland.

The Kilfenora Teaboy

I'm the Kilfenora teaboy
And I'm not so very young,
But though the land is going to pieces
I will not take up the gun;
I am happy making tea,
I make lots of it when I can,
And when I can't – I just make do;
And I do a small bit of sheepfarming on the side.

Oh but it's the small bit of furze between two towns
Is what makes the Kilfenora teaboy really run.

I have nine healthy daughters
And please God I will have more,
Sometimes my dear wife beats me
But on the whole she's a gentle soul;
When I'm not making her some tea
I sit out and watch them all
Ring-a-rosying in the street;
And I do a small bit of sheepfarming on the side.

Oh but it's the small bit of furze between two towns
Is what makes the Kilfenora teaboy really run.

Oh indeed my wife is handsome,
She has a fire lighting in each eye,
You can pluck laughter from her elbows
And from her knees pour money's tears;
I make all my tea for her,
I'm her teaboy on the hill,
And I also thatch her roof;
And I do a small bit of sheepfarming on the side.

Oh but it's the small bit of furze between two towns
Is what makes the Kilfenora teaboy really run.

And I'm not only a famous teaboy,
I'm a famous caveman too;
I paint pictures by the hundred
But you can't sell walls;
Although the people praise my pictures
As well as my turf-perfumèd blend
They rarely fling a fiver in my face;
Oh don't we do an awful lot of dying on the side?

But oh it's the small bit of furze between two towns
Is what makes the Kilfenora teaboy really run.

What is a Protestant, Daddy?

Gaiters were sinister
And you dared not
Glance up at the visage;
It was a long lean visage
With a crooked nose
And beaked dry lips
And streaky grey hair
And they used scurry about
In small black cars
(Unlike Catholic bishops
Stately in big cars
Or Pope Pius XII
In his gold-plated Cadillac)
And they'd make dashes for it
Across deserted streets
And disappear quickly
Into vast cathedrals
All silent and aloof,
Forlorn and leafless,
Their belfry louvres
Like dead men's lips,
And whose congregations, if any,
Were all octogenarian
With names like Iris;
More likely
There were no congregations
And these rodent-like clergymen
Were conspirators;
You could see it in their faces;
But as to what the conspiracies
Were about, as children
We were at a loss to know;
Our parents called them 'parsons'

Which turned them from being rodents
Into black hooded crows
Evilly flapping their wings
About our virginal souls;
And these 'parsons' had wives –
As unimaginable a state of affairs
As it would have been to imagine
A pope in a urinal;
Protestants were Martians
Light years more weird
Than zoological creatures;
But soon they would all go away
For as a species they were dying out,
Soon there would be no more Protestants . . .
Oh Yea, Oh Lord,
I was a proper little Irish Catholic boy
Way back in the 1950s.

Sam's Cross (1978)

Parents

A child's face is a drowned face:
Her parents stare down at her asleep
Estranged from her by a sea:
She is under the sea
And they are above the sea:
If she looked up she would see them
As if locked out of their own home,
Their mouths open,
Their foreheads furrowed –
Pursed-up orifices of fearful fish –
Their big ears are fins behind glass
And in her sleep she is calling out to them
    Father, Father
    Mother, Mother
But they cannot hear her:
She is inside the sea
And they are outside the sea.
Through the night, stranded, they stare
At the drowned, drowned face of their child.

Going Home to Mayo, Winter, 1949

Leaving behind us the alien, foreign city of Dublin,
My father drove through the night in an old Ford Anglia,
His five-year-old son in the seat beside him,
The rexine seat of red leatherette,
And a yellow moon peered in through the windscreen.
'Daddy, Daddy,' I cried, 'pass out the moon,'
But no matter how hard he drove he could not pass out the
    moon.
Each town we passed through was another milestone
And their names were magic passwords into eternity:
Kilcock, Kinnegad, Strokestown, Elphin,
Tarmonbarry, Tulsk, Ballaghaderreen, Ballavary;
Now we were in Mayo and the next stop was Turlough,
The village of Turlough in the heartland of Mayo,
And my father's mother's house, all oil lamps and women,
And my bedroom over the public bar below,
And in the morning cattle-cries and cock-crows:
Life's seemingly seamless garment gorgeously rent
By their screeches and bellowings. And in the evenings
I walked with my father in the high grass down by the river
Talking with him – an unheard-of thing in the city.

But home was not home and the moon could be no more
    outflanked
Than the daylight nightmare of Dublin City:
Back down along the canal we chugged into the city
And each lock-gate tolled our mutual doom;
And railings and palings and asphalt and traffic lights,
And blocks after blocks of so-called 'new' tenements –
Thousands of crosses of loneliness planted
In the narrowing grave of the life of the father;
In the wide, wide cemetery of the boy's childhood.

Backside to the Wind

A fourteen-year-old boy is out rambling alone
By the scimitar shores of Killala Bay
And he is dreaming of a French Ireland,
Backside to the wind.

What kind of village would I now be living in?
French vocabularies intertwined with Gaelic
And Irish women with French fathers,
Backsides to the wind.

The Ballina Road would become the Rue Humbert
And wine would be the staple drink of the people;
A staple diet of potatoes and wine,
Backsides to the wind.

Monsieur Duffy might be the harbourmaster
And Madame Duffy the mother of thirteen
Tiny philosophers to overthrow Maynooth,
Backsides to the wind.

Father Molloy might be a worker-priest
Up to his knees in manure at the cattle-mart;
And dancing and loving on the streets at evening
Backsides to the wind.

Jean Arthur Rimbaud might have grown up here
In a hillside terrace under the round tower;
Would he, like me, have dreamed of an Arabian Dublin,
Backside to the wind?

Garda Ned MacHale might now be a gendarme
Having hysterics at the crossroads;
Excommunicating male motorists, ogling females,
Backside to the wind.

I walk on, facing the village ahead of me,
A small concrete oasis in the wild countryside;
Not the embodiment of the dream of a boy,
Backside to the wind.

Seagulls and crows, priests and nuns,
Perch on the rooftops and steeples,
And their Anglo-American mores asphyxiate me,
Backside to the wind.

Not to mention the Japanese invasion:
Blunt people as solemn as ourselves
And as humourless; money is our God,
Backside to the wind.

The medieval Franciscan Friary of Moyne
Stands house-high, roofless, by;
Past it rolls a vast asphalt pipe,
Backside to the wind,

Ferrying chemical waste out to sea
From the Asahi synthetic-fibre plant;
Where once monks sang, wage-earners slave,
Backsides to the wind.

Run on, sweet River Moy,
Although I end my song; you are
The scales of a salmon of a boy,
Backside to the wind.

Yet I have no choice but to leave, to leave,
And yet there is nowhere I more yearn to live
Than in my own wild countryside,
Backside to the wind.

1976

Making Love Outside Áras an Uachtaráin

When I was a boy, myself and my girl
Used bicycle up to the Phoenix Park;
Outside the gates we used lie in the grass
Making love outside Áras an Uachtaráin.

Often I wondered what de Valera would have thought
Inside in his ivory tower
If he knew that we were in his green, green grass
Making love outside Áras an Uachtaráin.

Because the odd thing was – oh how odd it was –
We both revered Irish patriots
And we dreamed our dreams of a green, green flag
Making love outside Áras an Uachtaráin.

But even had our names been Diarmaid and Gráinne
We doubted de Valera's approval
For a poet's son and a judge's daughter
Making love outside Áras an Uachtaráin.

I see him now in the heat-haze of the day
Blindly stalking us down;
And, levelling an ancient rifle, he says 'Stop
Making love outside Áras an Uachtaráin.'

Sister Agnes Writes to Her Belovèd Mother

Dear Mother, thank you for the egg cosy;
Sister Alberta (from near Clonakilty)
Said it was the nicest, positively the nicest,
Egg cosy she had ever seen. Here
The big news is that Rev. Mother is pregnant;
The whole convent is simply delighted;
We don't know who the lucky father is
But we have a shrewd idea who it might be:
Do you remember that Retreat Director
I wrote to you about? – The lovely old Jesuit
With a rosy nose – We think it was he –
So shy and retiring, just the type;
Fr P. J. Pegasus SJ.
Of course, it's all hush-hush,
Nobody is supposed to know anything
In case the Bishop – that young hypocrite –
Might get to hear about it.
When her time comes Rev. Mother officially
Will go away on retreat
And the cherub will be reared in another convent.
But, considering the general decline in vocations,
We are all pleased as pea-shooters
That God has blessed the Order of the Little Tree
With another new sapling, all of our own making,
And of Jesuit pedigree, too.
Nevertheless – not a word.
Myself, I am crocheting a cradle shawl;
Hope you're doing your novenas. Love, Aggie.

Jesus, Break His Fall (1980)

The Death by Heroin of Sid Vicious

There – but for the clutch of luck – go I.

At daybreak – in the arctic fog of a February daybreak –
Shoulder-length helmets in the watchtowers of the
        concentration camp
Caught me out in the intersecting arcs of the swirling
        searchlights.

There were at least a zillion of us caught out there –
Like ladybirds under a boulder –
But under the microscope each of us was unique,

Unique and we broke for cover, crazily breasting
The barbed wire and some of us made it
To the forest edge, but many of us did not

Make it, although their unborn children did –
Such as you whom the camp commandant branded
Sid Vicious of the Sex Pistols. Jesus, break his fall:

There – but for the clutch of luck – go we all.

February 1979

The Drimoleague Blues

to Sarah and Síabhra

Oh I know this mean town is not always mean
And I know that you do not always mean what you mean
And the meaning of meaning can both mean and not
    mean:
But I mean to say, I mean to say,
I've got the Drimoleague Blues, I've got the Drimoleague
    Blues,
I've got the Drimoleague Blues so bad I can't move:
Even if you were to plug in Drimoleague to every oil well in
    Arabia –
I'd still have the Drimoleague Blues.

Oh this town is so mean that it's got its own mean
And that's to be as mean as green, as mean as green:
Shoot a girl dead and win yourself a bride,
Shoot a horse dead and win yourself a car.
Oh I've got the Drimoleague Blues, I've got the Drimoleague
    Blues,
I've got the Drimoleague Blues so bad I can't move:
Even if you were to plug in Drimoleague to every oil well in
    Arabia –
I'd still have the Drimoleague Blues.

And so on right down to the end of the line
Mean with Mean will always rhyme
And Man with Man: Oh where is the Woman
With the Plough, where is her Daughter with the Stars?
Oh I've got the Drimoleague Blues, I've got the Drimoleague
    Blues,
I've got the Drimoleague Blues so bad I can't move:
Even if you were to plug in Drimoleague to every oil well in
    Arabia –
I'd still have the Drimoleague Blues.

Tullynoe: Tête-à-Tête in the Parish Priest's Parlour

'Ah, he was a grand man.'
'He was: he fell out of the train going to Sligo.'
'He did: he thought he was going to the lavatory.'
'He did: in fact he stepped out the rear door of the train.'
'He did: God, he must have got an awful fright.'
'He did: he saw that it wasn't the lavatory at all.'
'He did: he saw that it was the railway tracks going away from
    him.'
'He did: I wonder if . . . but he was a grand man.'
'He was: he had the most expensive Toyota you can buy.'
'He had: well, it was only beautiful.'
'It was: he used to have an Audi.'
'He had: as a matter of fact he used to have two Audis.'
'He had: and then he had an Avenger.'
'He had: and then he had a Volvo.'
'He had: in the beginning he had a lot of Volkses.'
'He had: he was a great man for the Volkses.'
'He was: did he once have an Escort?'
'He had not: he had a son a doctor.'
'He had: and he had a Morris Minor too.'
'He had: he had a sister a hairdresser in Kilmallock.'
'He had: he had another sister a hairdresser in Ballybunion.'
'He had: he was put in a coffin which was put in his father's cart.'
'He was: his lady wife sat on top of the coffin driving the donkey.'
'She did: Ah, but he was a grand man.'
'He was: he was a grand man . . .'
'Good night, Father.'
'Good night, Mary.'

En Famille, 1979

Bring me back to the dark school – to the dark school of
   childhood:
To where tiny is tiny, and massive is massive.

Jumping the Train Tracks with Angela (1983)

Interview for a Job

– I had a nervous breakdown when I was seventeen.
– You had not?
– I had.
– But how could a beautiful girl like you
    Have had such a thing as a nervous breakdown?
– I don't know, sir.
– But you have such luscious hair!
– They said I had some kind of depression.
– With long black curls like yours? Depression?
– Erogenous depression.
– Erogenous depression?
– It's a new kind of depression, sir.
– You're wearing clothes, do you know that?
– Am I?
– You are: I like your lips too.
– My lips?
– Your lips: they're kissable.
– Kissable?
– And your hips: I would say they handle well.
– I beg your pardon, sir?
– Tell me, what kind of man is your father?
– He stays in bed every second week.
– Your mother?
– She stays in bed every second week as well.
– A happy Irish marriage.
– Why do you say that, sir?
– Well, it's not every husband and wife who go to bed together
    For a whole week, every second week.
– You misunderstand, sir; they take it in turns.
– OK: so you want a job?
– Yes, sir.
– Well you can't have one.
– I beg your pardon, sir?

– You had one hell of a nerve applying for a job.
  You have no right to have a job here or anywhere.
  Get out of my office before I bellow for my Little Willie
  To kick you in the buck teeth and whack you on the bottom.
– Thank you verra much, sir.
– Don't mention it, girrul.
– Well then, sir, d'ye mind if I sit on in your office for five minutes:
  It is terrible cold outside and I have no overcoat.
– Bloody woman, shag off; vamoose; make yourself scarce.
– But sir, I *am* scarce; my name on the form . . . *Scarcity*.
– Now *Scarcity*, don't act the smart ass with me: beat it.

The Berlin Wall Café (1985)

The Haulier's Wife Meets Jesus on the Road Near Moone

I live in the town of Cahir,
In the Glen of Aherlow,
Not far from Peekaun
In the townland of Toureen,
At the foot of Galtee Mór
In the County of Tipperary.
I am thirty-three years old,
In the prime of my womanhood:
The mountain stream of my sex
In spate and darkly foaming;
The white hills of my breasts
Brimful and breathing;
The tall trees of my eyes
Screening blue skies;
Yet in each palm of my hand
A sheaf of fallen headstones.
When I stand in profile
Before my bedroom mirror
With my hands on my hips in my slip,
Proud of my body,
Unashamed of my pride,
I appear to myself a naked stranger,
A woman whom I do not know
Except fictionally in the looking-glass,
Quite dramatically beautiful.
Yet in my soul I yearn for affection,
My soul is empty for the want of affection.
I am married to a haulier,
A popular and a wealthy man,
An alcoholic and a county councillor,
Father with me of four sons,
By repute a sensitive man and he is
Except when he makes love to me:

He takes leave of his senses,
Handling me as if I were a sack of gravel
Or a carnival dummy,
A fruit machine or a dodgem.
He makes love to me about twice a year;
Thereafter he does not speak to me for weeks,
Sometimes not for months.
One night in Cruise's Hotel in Limerick
I whispered to him: Please *take* me.
(We had been married five years
And we had two children.)
Christ, do you know what he said?
Where? Where do you want me to take you?
And he rolled over and fell asleep,
Tanked up with seventeen pints of beer.
We live in a Georgian, Tudor, Classical Greek,
Moorish, Spanish Hacienda, Regency Period,
Ranch House, Three-Storey Bungalow
On the edge of the edge of town:
'Poor Joe's Row'
The townspeople call it,
But our real address is 'Ronald Reagan Hill' –
That vulturous-looking man in the States.
We're about twelve miles from Ballyporeen
Or, as the vulture flies, about eight miles.
After a month or two of silence
He says to me: Wife, I'm sorry;
I know that we should be separated,
Annulled or whatever,
But on account of the clients and the neighbours,
Not to mention the children, it is plain
As a pikestaff we are glued to one another
Until death do us part.
Why don't you treat yourself

To a weekend up in Dublin,
A night out at the theatre:
I'll pay for the whole shagging lot.

There was a play on at the time
In the Abbey Theatre in Dublin
Called *The Gigli Concert*,
And, because I liked the name –
But also because it starred
My favourite actor, Tom Hickey –
I telephoned the Abbey from Cahir.
They had but one vacant seat left!
I was so thrilled with myself,
And at the prospect of Tom Hickey
In a play called *The Gigli Concert*
(Such a euphonious name for a play, I thought),
That one wet day I drove over to Clonmel
And I went wild, and I bought a whole new outfit.
I am not one bit afraid to say
That I spent all of £200 on it
(Not, of course, that Tom Hickey would see me
But I'd be seeing myself seeing Tom Hickey
Which would be almost, if not quite,
The very next best thing):
A long, tight-fitting, black skirt
Of Chinese silk,
With matching black jacket
And lace-frilled, pearl-white blouse;
Black fishnet stockings with sequins;
Black stiletto high-heeled shoes
Of pure ostrich leather.
I thought to myself – subconsciously, of course –
If I don't transpose to be somebody's *femme fatale*
It won't anyhow be for the want of trying.

Driving up to Dublin I began to daydream
And either at Horse & Jockey or Abbeyleix
I took a wrong turn and within a quarter of an hour
I knew I was lost. I stopped the car
And I asked the first man I saw on the road
For directions:
'Follow me' – he said – 'my name is Jesus:
Have no fear of me – I am a travelling actor.
We'll have a drink together in the nearby inn.'
It turned out we were on the road near Moone.
(Have you ever been to the Cross at Moone?
Once my children and I had a picnic at Moone
When they were little and we were on one
Of our Flight into Egypt jaunts to Dublin.
They ran round the High Cross round and round
As if it were a maypole, which maybe it is:
Figure carvings of loaves and fishes, lions and dolphins.
I drank black coffee from a Thermos flask
And the children drank red lemonade
And they were wearing blue duffle coats with red scarves
And their small, round, laughing, freckled faces
Looked pointedly like the faces of the twelve apostles
Gazing out at us from the plinth of the Cross
Across a thousand years.
Only, of course, their father was not with us:
He was busy – busy being our family euphemism.
Every family in Ireland has its own family euphemism
Like a heraldic device or a coat of arms.)
Jesus turned out to be a lovely man,
All that a woman could ever possibly dream of:
Gentle, wild, soft-spoken, courteous, sad;
Angular, awkward, candid, methodical;
Humorous, passionate, angry, kind;
Entirely sensitive to a woman's world.
Discreetly I invited Jesus to spend the night with me –

Stay with me, the day is almost over and it is getting dark –
But he waved me aside with one wave of his hand,
Not contemptuously, but compassionately.
'Our night will come,' he smiled,
And he resumed chatting about my children,
All curiosity for their welfare and well-being.
It was like a fire burning in me when he talked to me.
There was only one matter I felt guilty about
And that was my empty vacant seat in the Abbey.
At closing time he kissed me on both cheeks
And we bade one another goodbye and then –
Just as I had all but given up hope –
He kissed me full on the mouth,
My mouth wet with alizarin lipstick
(A tube of Guerlain 4 which I've had for twelve years).
As I drove on into Dublin to the Shelbourne Hotel
I kept hearing his Midlands voice
Saying to me over and over, across the Garden of Gethsemane –
Our night will come.

Back in the town of Cahir,
In the Glen of Aherlow,
Not far from Peekaun
In the townland of Toureen,
At the foot of Galtee Mór
In the County of Tipperary,
For the sake of something to say
In front of our four sons
My husband said to me:
Well, what was Benjamino Gigli like?
Oh, 'twas a phenomenal concert!
And what was Tom Hickey like?
Miraculous – I whispered – miraculous.
Our night will come – he had smiled – our night will come.

High-Speed Car Wash

We were making love in the high-speed car wash
When a peculiar thing occurred:
When I chanced to glance around
As we were readjusting our seat belts,
I saw two nuns
Peering in the back window of my new Peugeot!
They were not aware that I could see them.
Their faces were suffused in a golden red
Sanctuary light as they stared in at us entranced:
The plush, emerald, furry rollers of the car wash
Plied, wheeled, shuddered, backwards – forwards,
Crawling all over the body of the car.
We let ourselves be clawed in it, and by it,
Surrendering ourselves to it;
Immersed, and yet not immersed, in its floods and suds,
Flowing into one another like Christ flowing into the Cross,
In one another's throats soaking together.

As we drove off, the car was dripping wet;
The two nuns in black gleaming in the sun,
Each with, in her hands behind her back,
A rolled-up red umbrella twirling to and fro,
Snatches of converse floating on the air:
– It's a lovely-looking car, really, isn't it, the new Peugeot?
– Oh it is . . . I thought it looked lovely in the car wash.
And I said to Maeve Smith: Maria Callas –
        didn't she really have a truly divine voice?
And Maeve Smith said to me: Yes, but do you know
        that her real name was Maria Anna Kalageropoulos?

Bob Dylan Concert at Slane, 1984

'I saw close up the make-up on Bob Dylan's face!'
She confides into the dressing-table looking glass in our
    bedroom,
Randy to report the felicity of what's morbid:
Mock-shock, sex-scandal, night-delight.

I glimpse the drenched pair of hips –
The drenched denimed pair of hips
Of the boy who, swimming across the river to get in,
Drowned. And while Bob Dylan and his band –
And a hundred thousand fans –
Made noise that out-Táined the Táin,
The St John of Malta Ambulance Women
Fished out a corpse –
Cradled it in a stretcher and wrapped it round
In grey swaddling – prison issue.

They offloaded him into the White Ambulance,
As into a Black Maria, then off and away – with him –
To begin a life sentence
For which there is no parole – no parole at all.
Not for nothing do men wear make-up
And poets earrings: not for nothing
Was Bob Dylan's noise noise, his music music.

The Cabinet Table

Alice Gunn is a cleaner woman
Down at Government Buildings,
And after seven o'clock Mass last night
(Isn't it a treat to be able to go to Sunday Mass
On a Saturday! To sit down to Saturday Night TV
Knowing you've fulfilled your Sunday obligation!)
She came back over to The Flats for a cup of tea
(I offered her sherry but she declined –
Oh, I never touch sherry on a Saturday night –
Whatever she meant by that, I don't know).
She had us in stitches, telling us
How one afternoon after a Cabinet Meeting
She got one of the security men
To lie down on the Cabinet Table,
And what she didn't do to him –
And what she did do to him –
She didn't half tell us;
But she told us enough to be going on with.
'Do you know what it is?' she says to me:
'No,' says I, 'what is it?'
'It's mahogany,' she says, 'pure mahogany.'

Hymn to a Broken Marriage

Dear Nessa – Now that our marriage is over
I would like you to know that, if I could put back the clock
Fifteen years to the cold March day of our wedding,
I would wed you again and, if that marriage also broke,
I would wed you yet again and, if it a third time broke,
Wed you again, and again, and again, and again, and again:
If you would have me which, of course, you would not.
For, even you – in spite of your patience and your innocence
(Strange characteristics in an age such as our own) –
Even you require to shake off the addiction of romantic love
And seek, instead, the herbal remedy of a sane affection
In which are mixed in profuse and fair proportion
Loverliness, brotherliness, fatherliness:
A sane man could not espouse a more intimate friend than you.

'Windfall', 8 Parnell Hill, Cork

But, then, at the end of day I could always say –
Well, now, I am going home.
I felt elected, steeped, sovereign to be able to say –
I am going home.
When I was at home I liked to stay at home;
At home I stayed at home for weeks;
At home I used sit in a winged chair by the window
Overlooking the river and the factory chimneys,
The electricity power station and the car assembly works,
The fleets of trawlers and the pilot tugs,
Dreaming that life is a dream which is real,
The river a reflection of itself in its own waters,
Goya sketching Goya among the smoky mirrors.
The industrial vista was my Mont Sainte-Victoire.
While my children sat on my knees watching TV
Their mother, my wife, reclined on the couch
Knitting a bright-coloured scarf, drinking a cup of black coffee,
Smoking a cigarette – one of her own roll-ups.
I closed my eyes and breathed in and breathed out.
It is ecstasy to breathe if you are at home in the world.
What a windfall! A home of our own!
Our neighbours' houses had names like 'Con Amore',
'Sans Souci', 'Pacelli', 'Montini', 'Homesville'.
But we called our home 'Windfall'.
'Windfall', 8 Parnell Hill, Cork.
In the gut of my head coursed the leaf of tranquillity
Which I dreamed was known only to Buddhist Monks
In lotus monasteries high up in the Hindu Kush.
Down here in the dark depths of Ireland,
Below sea level in the city of Cork,
In a city as intimate and homicidal as a Little Marseilles,
In a country where all the children of the nation
Are not cherished equally

And where the best go homeless, while the worst
Erect block-house palaces – self-regardingly ugly –
Having a home of your own can give to a family
A chance in a lifetime to transcend death.

At the high window, shipping from all over the world
Being borne up and down the busy, yet contemplative, river;
Skylines drifting in and out of skylines in the cloudy valley;
Firelight at dusk, and city lights;
Beyond them the control tower of the airport on the hill –
A lighthouse in the sky flashing green to white to green;
Our black-and-white cat snoozing in the corner of a chair;
Pastels and etchings on the four walls, and over the mantelpiece
'Van Gogh's Grave' and 'Lovers in Water';
A room wallpapered in books and family photograph albums
Chronicling the adventures and metamorphoses of family life:
In swaddling clothes in Mammy's arms on baptism day;
Being a baby of nine months and not remembering it;
Face-down in a pram, incarcerated in a high chair;
Everybody, including strangers, wearing shop-window smiles;
With Granny in Felixstowe, with Granny in Ballymaloe;
In a group photo in First Infants, on a bike at thirteen;
In the back garden in London, in the back garden in Cork;
Performing a headstand after First Holy Communion;
Getting a kiss from the Bishop on Confirmation Day;
Straw hats in the Bois de Boulougne, wearing wings at the
        seaside;
Mammy and Daddy holding hands on the Normandy Beaches;
Mammy and Daddy at the wedding of Jeremiah and Margot;
Mammy and Daddy queueing up for *Last Tango in Paris*;
Boating on the Shannon, climbing mountains in Kerry;
Building sandcastles in Killala, camping in Barley Cove;
Picnicking in Moone, hide-and-go-seek in Clonmacnoise;
Riding horses, cantering, jumping fences;
Pushing out toy yachts in the pond in the Tuileries;

The Irish College revisited in the Rue des Irlandais;
Sipping an *orange pressé* through a straw on the roof of the
	Beaubourg;
Dancing in Père Lachaise, weeping at Auvers.
Year in, year out, I pored over these albums accumulating,
My children looking over my shoulder, exhilarated as I was,
Their mother presiding at our ritual from a distance –
The far side of the hearthrug, diffidently, proudly.
Schoolbooks on the floor and pyjamas on the couch –
Whose turn is it tonight to put the children to bed?

Our children swam about our home
As if it was their private sea,
Their own unique, symbiotic fluid
Of which their parents also partook.
Such is home – a sea of your own –
In which you hang upside down from the ceiling
With equanimity, while postcards from Thailand on the
	mantelpiece
Are raising their eyebrow markings benignly:
Your hands dangling their prayers to the floorboards of your
	home,
Sifting the sands underneath the surfaces of conversations,
The marine insect life of the family psyche.
A home of your own – or a sea of your own –
In which climbing the walls is as natural
As making love on the stairs;
In which when the telephone rings
Husband and wife are metamorphosed into smiling accomplices,
Both declining to answer it;
Initiating, instead, a yet more subversive kiss –
A kiss they have perhaps never attempted before –
And might never have dreamed of attempting
Were it not for the telephone belling.
Through the bannisters or along the bannister rails

The pyjama-clad children solemnly watching
Their parents at play, jumping up and down in support,
Race back to bed, gesticulating wordlessly:
The most subversive unit in society is the human family.

We're almost home, pet, almost home . . .
Our home is at . . .
I'll be home . . .
I have to go home now . . .
I want to go home now . . .
Are you feeling homesick?
Are you anxious to get home? . . .
I can't wait to get home . . .
Let's stay at home tonight and . . .
What time will you be coming home at? . . .
If I'm not home by six at the latest, I'll phone . . .
We're nearly home, don't worry, we're nearly home . . .

But then with good reason
I was put out of my home:
By a keen wind felled.
I find myself now without a home
Having to live homeless in the alien, foreign city of Dublin.
It is an eerie enough feeling to be homesick
Yet knowing you will be going home next week;
It is an eerie feeling beyond all ornithological analysis
To be homesick knowing that there is no home to go home to:
Day by day, creeping, crawling,
Moonlighting, escaping,
Bed-and-breakfast to bed-and-breakfast;
Hostels, centres, one-night hotels.

Homeless in Dublin,
Blown about the suburban streets at evening,
Peering in the windows of other people's homes,

Wondering what it must feel like
To be sitting around a fire –
Apache or Cherokee or Bourgeoisie –
Beholding the firelit faces of your family,
Beholding their starry or their TV gaze:
Windfall to Windfall – can you hear me?
Windfall to Windfall . . .
We're almost home, pet, don't worry anymore, we're almost
    home.

Raymond of the Rooftops

The morning after the night
The roof flew off the house
And our sleeping children narrowly missed
Being decapitated by falling slates,
I asked my husband if he would
Help me put back the roof:
But no – he was too busy at his work
Writing for a women's magazine in London
An Irish fairytale called *Raymond of the Rooftops*.
Will you have a heart, woman – he bellowed –
Can't you see I am up to my eyes and ears in work,
Breaking my neck to finish *Raymond of the Rooftops*,
Fighting against time to finish *Raymond of the Rooftops*,
Putting everything I have got into *Raymond of the Rooftops*?

Isn't is well for him? *Everything he has got!*

All I wanted him to do was to stand
For an hour, maybe two hours, three at the most,
At the bottom of the stepladder
And hand me up slates while I slated the roof:
But no – once again I was proving to be the insensitive,
Thoughtless, feckless even, wife of the artist.
There was I up to my fat, raw knees in rainwater
Worrying him about the hole in our roof
While he was up to his neck in *Raymond of the Rooftops*.
Will you have a heart, woman – he bellowed –
Can't you see I am up to my eyes and ears in work,
Breaking my neck to finish *Raymond of the Rooftops*,
Fighting against time to finish *Raymond of the Rooftops*,
Putting everything I have got into *Raymond of the Rooftops*?

Isn't it well for him? *Everything he has got!*

The Pièta's Over

The Pièta's over – and, now, my dear, droll husband,
As middle age tolls its bell along the via dolorosa of life,
It is time for you to get down off my knees
And learn to walk on your own two feet.
I will admit it is difficult for a man of forty
Who has spent all his life reclining in his wife's lap,
Being given birth to by her again and again, year in, year out,
To stand on his own two feet, but it has to be done –
Even if at the end of the day he commits hari-kari.
A man cannot be a messiah for ever,
Messiahing about in his wife's lap,
Suffering fluently in her arms,
Flowing up and down in the lee of her bosom,
Forever being mourned for by the eternal feminine,
Being keened over every night of the week for sixty mortal
        years.

The Pièta's over – it is Easter over all our lives:
The revelation of our broken marriage, and its resurrection;
The breaking open of the tomb, and the setting free.
Painful as it was for me, I put you down off my knee
And I showed you the door.
Although you pleaded with me to keep you on my knee
And to mollycoddle you, humour you, within the family circle
('Don't put me out into the cold world,' you cried),
I did not take the easy way out and yield to you.
Instead I took down the door off its hinges
So that the sunlight shone all the more squarely
Upon the pure, original brokenness of our marriage;
I whispered to you, quietly, yet audibly,
For all the diaspora of your soul to hear:
The Pièta's over.

Yet even now, one year later, you keep looking back
From one side of Europe to the other,
Gaping at my knees as if my knees
Were the source of all that you have been, are, or will be.
By all means look around you, but stop looking back.
I would not give you shelter if you were homeless in the streets
For you must make your home in yourself, not in a woman.
Keep going out the road for it is only out there –
Out there where the river achieves its riverlessness –
That you and I can become at last strangers to one another,
Ready to join up again on Resurrection Day.
Therefore, I must keep whispering to you, over and over:
My dear loved one, I have to tell you,
You have run the gamut of piety –
The Pièta's over.

The Berlin Wall Café

Once we were Berlin – you and I . . .
Until an agèd priest,
As shepherdlike a pastor as one could hope to meet
In the neon forest –
Father Boniface –
Married us with a gun.
Tears of joy were in his eyes as, with a flick of his wrist
(All mottled and bluey),
He waved his pistol in the air, firing gaily:
A long white wall unfurled from it,
Trailing its roll-top and its graffiti.

Thus it was we pitched our tent in the continuing city:
Ecstatically lonely together in a two-room flat
In Bernauer Strasse beside the Berlin Wall,
Around the corner from the open-air table tennis tables
In Swinemünder Strasse,
Handy for the *U-Bahn* in Volta Strasse.
I counted myself the luckiest man alive in Berlin
To be marooned with you:
You – incarnate coincidence of the beautiful and the true –
All risk and give –
Reticent woman whose eyes were caves
Concealed in cascades of red hair.
Yet all I could talk about was the Berlin Wall,
As if the Berlin Wall was more important than you!
On the night you gave birth to our child
I was too busy to attend – addressing a meeting
On the Berlin Wall!
When I should have been cooking your supper
After your long day's work in the office in Spandau,
I was manning the Observation Platforms –
Making faces at the *Volkspolizei*!

At the end of 1980,
When I should have been minding our marriage
And concentrating on loving you,
All I could consider was whether or not
I should become Editor of the *Berlin Wall Gazette*:
I was a most proper Charlie!
No wonder that your friends could not abide me!
Whenever they saw me approaching they scattered:
'Watch out – here he comes – Checkpoint Charlie.'

In 1984 you could stand it no more:
You escaped from West Berlin
Into East Berlin – where you are free of me
And of the Show Biz of the Free Democracies
Advertising Unemployment and All That Jazz.
Purple with envy, I hear you have teamed up
With an all-woman jazz combo in Unter den Linden.
They say there's no more exciting woman in Berlin
Than when you're alone on the high-hat cymbals
To beat the band in the Berlin Wall Café:
Once we were Berlin . . . you and I . . .

At the Funeral of the Marriage

At the funeral of the marriage
My wife and I paced
On either side of the hearse,
Our children racing behind it . . .
As the coffin was emptied
Down into the bottomless grave,
Our children stood in a half-circle,
Playing on flutes and recorders.
My wife and I held hands.
While the mourners wept and the gravediggers
Unfurled shovelfuls of clay
Down on top of the coffin,
We slowly walked away,
Accomplices beneath the yew trees.
We had a cup of tea in the graveyard café
Across the street from the gates:
We discussed the texture of the undertaker's face,
Its beetroot quality.
As I gazed at my wife
I wondered who on earth she was –
I saw that she was a green-eyed stranger.
I said to her: Would you like to go to a film?
She said: I would love to go to a film.
In the back seats of the cinema,
As we slid up and down in our seats
In a frenzy of hooks and clasps,
The manager courteously asked us not to take off our clothes.
We walked off urgently through the rain-strewn streets
Into a leaf-sodden cul-de-sac
And as, from the tropic isle of our bed,
Chock-a-block with sighs and cries,

We threw our funeral garments on the floor,
We could hear laughter outside the door.
There is no noise children love more to hear
Than the noise of their parents making love:
O my darling, who on earth are you?

Going Home to Russia (1987)

Cardinal Dies of Heart Attack in Dublin Brothel

Edifying, edifying – you cry – edifying –
As in silence we sit listening to the six o'clock TV news
That our belovèd cardinal has died
In the arms of his favourite prostitute.
At last – I think to myself in the solitude of my soul –
A sign that the Church of God is moving into the light.

I put on my overcoat and, as there are rainclouds,
I take the precaution of bringing along my umbrella.
I have to walk the long way round to the church
Whose candlelit darkness proves always consoling.
I insert a 50p piece in the moneybox and light three candles:
One for the Cardinal, one for the Lady,
And one for the Unknown Soldier in all of us.
I kneel down in a pew to pray
But I quickly translate myself into a sitting position.
The sitting position is my natural position.
My soul is borne up on wings of flame
In which I think again of the agèd cardinal's submission
To that lovely, ephemeral woman
And of her compassion which, by all accounts,
Was as tender as it was fiery.
I depart the church, feeling restored in body and soul.
As you say, my dear wife, with your characteristic wit
And solicitude – our belovèd cardinal who has died in a brothel
Was, in the very last analysis, 'a broth of a cardinal'.

What Shall I Wear, Darling, to *The Great Hunger*?

'What shall I wear, darling, to *The Great Hunger*?'
She shrieked at me helplessly from the east bedroom
Where the west wind does be blowing betimes.
I did not hesitate to hazard a spontaneous response:
'Your green evening gown –
Your see-through, sleeveless, backless, green evening gown.'
We arrived at the Peacock
In good time for everybody to have a good gawk at her
Before the curtain went up on *The Great Hunger*.
At the interval everybody was clucking about, cooing
That it was simply stunning – her dress –
'Darling, you look like Mother Divinity in your see-through,
Sleeveless, backless, green evening gown – it's so visual!'
At the party after the show – simply everybody was there –
Winston Lenihan, Consolata O'Carroll-Riviera, Yves St Kiekegaard –
She was so busy being admired that she forgot to get drunk.
But the next morning it was business as usual –
Grey serge pants, blue donkey jacket – driving around Dolphin's
    Barn
In her Opel Kadett hatchback
Checking up on the rents. 'All these unmarried young mothers
And their frogspawn, living on the welfare –
You would think that it never occurs to them
That it's their rents that pay for the outfits I have to wear
Whenever *The Great Hunger* is playing at the Peacock.
No, it never occurs to them that in Ireland today
It is not easy to be a landlord and a patron of the arts.
It is not for nothing that we in Fail Gael have a social conscience:
Either you pay the shagging rent or you get out on the street.
Next week I have to attend three-and-a-half *Great Hungers*,
Not to mention a half-dozen *Juno and the Paycocks*.'

The Divorce Referendum, Ireland, 1986

By the time the priest started into his sermon
I was adrift on a leaf of tranquillity,
Feeling only the need and desire to praise,
To feed praise to the tiger of life.
Hosanna, Hosanna, Hosanna.
He was a gentle-voiced, middle-aged man,
Slightly stooped under a gulf of grey hair,
Slightly tormented by an excess of humility.
He talked felicitously of the Holy Spirit –
As if he really believed in what he was preaching –
Not as if he was aiming to annotate a diagram
Or to sub-edit the Gospel,
But as if the Holy Spirit was real as rainwater.
Then his voice changed colour –
You could see it change from pink into white.
He rasped: 'It is the wish of the Hierarchy
That today the clergy of Ireland put before you
Christ's teaching on the indissolubility of marriage
And to remind you that when you vote in the Divorce Referendum
The Church's teaching and Christ's teaching are one and the
        same.'
Stunned, I stared up at him from my pew
As he stood there supported by candles and gladioli,
Vestments, and altarboys at his feet;
I could feel my breastplate tighten and my shoulderblades quiver;
I knew the anger that Jesus Christ felt
When he drove from the temple the traders and stockbrokers.
I have come into this temple today to pray
And be healed by, and joined with, the Spirit of Life,
Not to be invaded by ideology.
I say unto you, preacher and orators of the Hierarchy,
Do not bring ideology into my house of prayer.

I closed my eyes
And I did not open them again until I could hear
The priest murmuring the prayers of the Consecration.
At Holy Communion I kept my eyes on a small girl
To whom the priest had to bend low to give her the host.
Curtseying, she smiled eagerly, and flew back down the aisle,
Carrying in her breast the Eucharist of her innocence:
May she have children of her own
And as many husbands as will praise her –
For what are husbands for, but to praise their wives?

A Vision of Africa on the Coast of Kerry

On the coast at Meenogahane,
Near Causeway,
Nellie presides in the kitchen of her cottage,
At eighty-five, exchanging the time of day
With tourists, educating us:
Nellie who has never in her life
Been out of her townland
Except 'the wanst'.
Five years ago at eighty,
When she had a stroke,
She was transported
By county ambulance
To the Regional Hospital in Cork.
Do you know what I saw there?
No, Nellie, what did you see?
I saw a black man.
A black man?
A black man – you should have seen his neck!
His neck?
Oh the neck of him – the lovely neck of him!
The lovely, wet, shiny, rubbery neck of him!
I asked him if he would let me put my hand on it
And he did, he let me –
And it was all black, do you know?
Oh it was lovely, I tell you, lovely!

Martha's Wall

Her pleasure – what gave her pleasure – was to be walked
Down her wall, the South Wall, a skinny, crinkly, golden-stemmed
 wall
That contracts and expands, worms and unworms, in and out of
 Dublin Bay,
Across the sea's thighs pillowing in, besotted, under daisy-gartered
 skies.
She'd curl her finger around my finger and I'd lead her out on to it.
She liked it when the flowering sea was shedding spray across it.
She'd tense up with delight to see me get wet
And wetter still, and wetter – the wetter it was
The better she liked it, and me – and she wanted always
To get down, away down, to the very end of it
Where there is a deep-red lighthouse, and the deep-red lighthouse
Was hers also, hers, and we'd sit down on a bench under it
And she'd put her arm around my neck and we'd stop needing to
 speak
And we'd sit there, breathless, in silence, for a long time.

Six Nuns Die in Convent Inferno

*To the
happy memory of six Loreto nuns
who died
between midnight and morning of
2 June 1986*

I

We resided in a Loreto convent in the centre of Dublin city
On the east side of a public gardens, St Stephen's Green.
Grafton Street – the *paseo*
Where everybody *paseo*'d, including even ourselves –
Debouched on the north side, and at the top of Grafton Street,
Or round the base of the great patriotic pebble of O'Donovan Rossa,
Knelt tableaus of punk girls and punk boys.
When I used pass them – scurrying as I went –
Often as not to catch a mass in Clarendon Street,
The Carmelite Church in Clarendon Street
(Myself, I never used the Clarendon Street entrance,
I always slipped in by way of Johnson's Court,
Opposite the side entrance to Bewley's Oriental Café),
I could not help but smile, as I sucked on a Fox's mint,
That for all the half-shaven heads and the martial garb
And the dyed hair-dos and the nappy pins
They looked so conventional, really, and vulnerable,
Clinging to warpaint and to uniforms and to one another.
I knew it was myself who was the ultimate drop-out,
The delinquent, the recidivist, the vagabond,
The wild woman, the subversive, the original punk.
Yet, although I confess I was smiling, I was also afraid,
Appalled by my own nerve, my own fervour,
My apocalyptic enthusiasm, my other-worldly hubris:
To opt out of the world and to
Choose such exotic loneliness,

Such terrestrial abandonment,
A lifetime of bicycle lamps and bicycle pumps,
A lifetime of galoshes stowed under the stairs,
A lifetime of umbrellas drying out in the kitchens.

I was an old nun – an agèd beadswoman –
But I was no daw.
I knew what a weird bird I was, I knew that when we
Went to bed we were as eerie an aviary as you'd find
In all the blown-off rooftops of the city:
Scuttling about our dorm, wheezing, shrieking, croaking,
In our yellowy corsets, wonky suspenders, strung-out garters,
A bony crew in the gods of the sleeping city.
Many's the night I lay awake in bed
Dreaming what would befall us if there were a fire:
No fire-escapes outside, no fire-extinguishers inside;
To coin a Dublin saying,
We'd not stand a snowball's chance in hell. Fancy that!
It seemed too good to be true:
Happy death vouchsafed only to the few.
Sleeping up there was like sleeping at the top of the mast
Of a nineteenth-century schooner, and in the daytime
We old nuns were the ones who crawled out on the yardarms
To stitch and sew the rigging and the canvas.
To be sure we were weird birds, oddballs, Christniks,
For we had done the weirdest thing a woman can do –
Surrendered the marvellous passions of girlhood,
The innocent dreams of childhood,
Not for a night or a weekend or even a Lent or a season,
But for a lifetime.
Never to know the love of a man or a woman;
Never to have children of our own;
Never to have a home of our own;
All for why and for what?
To follow a young man – would you believe it –

Who lived two thousand years ago in Palestine
And who died a common criminal strung up on a tree.

As we stood there in the disintegrating dormitory
Burning to death in the arms of Christ –
O Christ, Christ, come quickly, quickly –
Fluttering about in our tight, gold bodices,
Beating our wings in vain,
It reminded me of the snaps one of the sisters took
When we took a seaside holiday in 1956
(The year Cardinal Mindszenty went into hiding
In the US legation in Budapest.
He was a great hero of ours, Cardinal Mindszenty,
Any of us would have given our right arm
To have been his nun – darning his socks, cooking his meals,
Making his bed, doing his washing and ironing.)
Somebody – an affluent buddy of the bishop's repenting his
        affluence –
Loaned Mother Superior a secluded beach in Co. Waterford –
Ardmore, along the coast from Tramore –
A cove with palm trees, no less, well off the main road.
There we were, fluttering up and down the beach,
Scampering hither and thither in our starched bathing-costumes.
Tonight, expiring in the fire, was quite much like that,
Only instead of scampering into the waves of the sea,
Now we were scampering into the flames of the fire.

That was one of the gayest days of my life,
The day the sisters went swimming.
Often in the silent darkness of the chapel after Benediction,
During the Exposition of the Blessed Sacrament,
I glimpsed the sea again as it was that day.
Praying – daydreaming really –
I became aware that Christ is the ocean
Forever rising and falling on the world's shore.

Now tonight in the convent Christ is the fire in whose waves
We are doomed but delighted to drown.
And, darting in and out of the flames of the dormitory,
Gabriel, with that extraordinary message of his on his boyish lips,
Frenetically pedalling his skybike.
He whispers into my ear what I must do
And I do it – and die.
Each of us in our own tiny, frail, furtive way
Was a Mother of God, mothering forth illegitimate Christs
In the street life of Dublin city.
God have mercy on our whirring souls –
Wild women were we all –
And on the misfortunate, poor fire-brigade men
Whose task it will be to shovel up our ashes and shovel
What is left of us into black plastic refuse sacks.
Fire-brigade men are the salt of the earth.

Isn't it a marvellous thing how your hour comes
When you least expect it? When you lose a thing,
Not to know about it until it actually happens?
How, in so many ways, losing things is such a refreshing
          experience,
Giving you a sense of freedom you've not often experienced?
How lucky I was to lose – I say, lose – lose my life.
It was a Sunday night, and after vespers
I skipped bathroom so that I could hop straight into bed
And get in a bit of a read before lights out:
Conor Cruise O'Brien's new book *The Siege*,
All about Israel and superlatively insightful
For a man who they say is reputedly an agnostic –
I got a loan of it from the brother-in-law's married niece –
But I was tired out and I fell asleep with the book open
Face down across my breast and I woke
To the racket of bellowing flame and snarling glass.
The first thing I thought was that the brother-in-law's married niece

Would never again get her Conor Cruise O'Brien back
And I had seen on the price-tag that it cost £23.00:
Small wonder that the custom of snipping off the price
As an exercise in social deportment has simply died out;
Indeed a book today is almost worth buying for its price,
Its price frequently being more remarkable than its contents.

The strange Eucharist of my death –
To be eaten alive by fire and smoke.
I clasped the dragon to my breast
And stroked his red-hot ears.
Strange! There we were, all sleeping molecules,
Suddenly all giving birth to our deaths,
All frantically in labour.
Doctors and midwives weaved in and out
In gowns of smoke and gloves of fire.
Christ, like an Orthodox patriarch in his dressing gown,
Flew up and down the dormitory, splashing water on our souls:
Sister Eucharia; Sister Seraphia; Sister Rosario;
Sister Gonzaga; Sister Margaret; Sister Edith.
If you will remember us – six nuns burnt to death –
Remember us for the frisky girls that we were,
Now more than ever kittens in the sun.

II

When Jesus heard these words at the top of Grafton Street
Uttered by a small, agèd, emaciated, female punk
Clad all in mourning black, and grieving like an alley cat,
He was annulled with astonishment, and turning round
He declared to the gangs of teenagers and dicemen following him:
'I tell you, not even in New York City
Have I found faith like this.'

That night in St Stephen's Green,
After the keepers had locked the gates,
And the courting couples had found cinemas themselves to die in,
The six nuns who had died in the convent inferno,
From the bandstand they'd been hiding under, crept out
And knelt together by the Fountain of the Three Fates,
Reciting the Agnus Dei: reciting it as if it were the torch song
Of all aid – Live Aid, Self Aid, Aids, and All Aid –
Lord, I am not worthy
That thou should'st enter under my roof;
Say but the word and my soul shall be healed.

The Beckett at the Gate

to Derek Mahon

That spring in Dublin
You could not go anywhere
Without people barking at you,
Buttonholing you in the street and barking at you,
Accosting you and barking at you:
'Have you not seen Barry McGovern's Beckett?'
Or else, which was worse,
'Have you not been to the Beckett at the Gate?'
I was fed up with people barking at me:
'Have you not seen Barry McGovern's Beckett?
Have you not been to the Beckett at the Gate?'

'No, I have not seen Barry McGovern's Beckett –
No, I have not been to the Beckett at the Gate –'
I'd mutter, affecting
To look under my legs
As if it was I
Who was the weary, put-upon virtuoso of bathos,
My limp tail of ejection.
In any case, I am not mad
About going to the theatre,
Going alone to the theatre
Upon a gloomy night in May.
It was, therefore, in spite of myself,
Quite against the grain,
That I took the initiative
By booking a ticket
For a Tuesday night at the Gate
In the third week of May
For Barry McGovern's Beckett,
The Beckett at the Gate.
C9 was the number of my ticket,
Centre, third row from the front.

I got there in good time.
I like to get to a thing in good time
Whatever it is – the bus into town,
Or the bus back out of town –
With at least a quarter of an hour to spare,
Preferably half an hour, ample time
In which to work up an adequate steam of anxiety.
When I stepped into the auditorium
I was relieved to see it was near empty,
I was heartened to see
That it was near empty,
Four or five patrons
Scattered about the theatre.

Consoled, a little less disconcerted
By the general regatta,
A little less addled
By the whole regrettable adventure,
A little less regretful
That I had not stayed put
In my bedsit,
I made my way to my seat,
Only to discover that one
Of the four or five patrons
Scattered about the near-empty theatre
Transpired to be ensconced
In the adjacent tip-up seat
Right next to my own.
In silence we sat, side by side,
All the house-lights on,
For the entire fifteen minutes before curtain-up.
I felt a right, roaring idiot,
Crouched there in all that silence
In row C of the Gate
Shoulder to shoulder with that –

That other human being
A woman to boot,
A young woman to boot.

To make matters worse
She was more sprawled than seated,
More dispersed than disposed,
More horizontal than vertical,
Engrossed in a paperback book
The name of which by dint
Of craning of the neck
I did manage to pick out.
It was a Picador paperback
Entitled *One Hundred Years of Solitude*.
As if that was not bad enough
There was not enough leg-room;
So that I had to scrunch up my legs,
Thereby having to sit closer to her.
A minute before the performance began
Someone (obviously some kind of friend,
Some ilk of accomplice)
Hailed her from five rows back:
'Michelle, Michelle!'
I said to myself
If only Michelle's friends
Would invite Michelle to sit with them
Then I'd have all of row C
To myself which at least
Would make the next hour and a half
If not less of a cauchemar
At least a bearable cauchemar.
But no – Michelle stayed put
And the lights went out,
And the curtain up,
And I knew I was for it.

Why had I let myself
Be bothered and browbeaten
By all those cultural groupies
Going on, and on, and on,
'Have you not seen Barry McGovern's Beckett?
Have you not been to the Beckett at the Gate?'

Well, it was out of the top drawer,
As Joseph Holloway would have put it,
Or would not have put it.
Not since the Depression of the 1950s
And the clowns in Duffy's Circus
Have I laughed myself so sorry,
So sorry that I was ready to shout,
If anyone else had shouted:
'Stop Beckett! Stop McGovern!'

And Michelle? Well, Michelle –
I mean talk about Susannah,
Or Judith and Holofernes,
Or any or all of those females
In the Old Testament,
Sarah or Rachel or even Eve;
Not to mention the New Testament,
Martha or Mary or Magdalen –
Michelle was – well, Michelle.
All right, I ought to have said
She was exceptionally petite –
But it's a small point
And to dwell on it
Would detract from her own performance.
She gave herself over to her own laughter
To such an exuberant extent
That she was wholly inside it – within the orbit
Of her own transparent laughter,

All rouge and polythene.
Every time she laughed
She kicked me in the legs,
In the backs of my legs,
Or nudged me in the kneecaps –
Unintentionally, of course.
Abruptly, she sat up in her seat
Tucking her legs in under her bottom –
Crimson red booties, blue skin-tight jeans,
Airy black blouse.
She leaned her head on my shoulder,
As if we had been espoused for years,
Donkeys' years, camels' years, elephants' years.
Occasionally, at a particularly
Outrageous piece of malarkey
By Beckett-McGovern,
She'd grip my arm tight
And howl – luminously howl.
Well, obviously, things
Had got quite out of hand
And I wanted to say to her
'Please please please please
Go on doing what you're doing.'
But I did not say anything.
A mum's-the-word man
Is what I am;
Not a word to the Reverend Mother,
Not a smoke-signal to Chief Sitting Mountain.
If there was an interval – and it said
In the programme that there was
An interval of fifteen minutes –
I do not remember any interval.
All I remember is Michelle's head
On my shoulder, and the kick
Of her hair brushing against my cheekbone.

Many years had elapsed since last
I had been made aware of my cheekbone –
Her mousy hair brushing against it,
Scented, and wet, and calamitous.

When the curtain came down
And the applause had drained away
I turned around to gaze
In rapture at Michelle
But she had slipped away.
Mother of God
Chosen by the Eternal Council!
I walked back down along O'Connell Street,
Muttering to myself,
'Have you not seen Barry McGovern's Beckett?
Have you not been to the Beckett at the Gate?'
Every few steps, covertly,
I gave a kick in the air:
'Have you not seen Barry McGovern's Beckett?
Have you not been to the Beckett at the Gate?'
It was dusk – lucid,
Warm, limpid,
On O'Connell Street Bridge.
Spilling over with self-pity
And lasciviously gazing down
At the bicycle-filled waters
Of the River Liffey running on, on,
I elected to walk on
Back to my bedsit in Ringsend
(Instead of taking the bus)
Through the East European parts of Dublin City,
Past the gasometer and Grand Canal Dock,
Misery Hill, The Gut, The Drain,
The Three Locks, Camden, Buckingham, Westmoreland.
At Ringsend there was a full moon over

The Sugar Loaf and the Wicklow Hills,
And the crimson lights of the telecommunications aerial
On the Three Rock Mountain were trembling
And on the television transmitter in Donnybrook;
And the hand-painted signs of the local public houses,
FitzHarris's and The Oarsman,
Looked childmade in the lamplight, homely
By the River Dodder,
As I balanced in a trance on the humpbacked bridge,
On a fulcrum of poignancy,
And I felt like a stranger in a new city,
An urchin in a New Jerusalem,
A bareheaded protagonist
In a vision of reality,
All caught up in a huge romance,
In a hot erotic cold tumult.
On the street corner in Ringsend village
Not at, but close to, a bus stop,
A tiny young woman was standing,
Hovering, twirling, stamping,
And when I saw that it was Michelle –
As I passed her by
She scrutinized me serenely
As if she had never seen me before –
As if she had never seen me before.
I keep on walking;
I'll go on, I think, I'll go on.
Next year in Carrickmines
I'll play tennis with whatever
Woman will play tennis with me
And I'll never be never again.
Next year in Carrickmines.
On grass. Love all.
Fifteen Love. Thirty Love. Forty Love.
Deuce. Advantage Miss Always.

Game, Set and Match.
Why you, Michelle? why you?
Will you join me? Join me?
If you're the joining kind, please join me.
Next year in Carrickmines,
Greystones, Delgany, Killiney, Bray, Dalkey, Shankill, Kilmacud,
Galloping Green, Stillorgan – perhaps even Dublin.

There's a beckett at the gate, there's a beckett
         at the gate, Michelle;
There's a Beckett at the gate, there's a Beckett
         at the gate, Michelle;
There's a beckett at the Gate, there's a beckett
         at the Gate, Michelle;
There's a Beckett at the Gate, there's a Beckett
         at the Gate, Michelle.

Hymn to my Father

Dear Daddy, on your last legs now,
Can you hear me
In your bedroom in the treetops,
Chained to your footwarmer and your pills,
Death notices in newspapers your exclusive reading?
We had no life together – or almost none.
Yet you made me what I am –
A man in search of his Russia.
After schooldays I became a poet –
A metamorphosis you could no more fathom
Than I could fathom your own osmosis –
Lawyer with a secret life,
As secret as the life of a poet.
You had a history for every milestone,
A saga for every place name –
The Bovril Sign, the Ballast Office Clock, the Broadstone –
And so, at your knee, at your elbow, I became you.
Estranged as we are,
I am glad that it was in this life
I loved you,
Not the next.
O Russian Knight at the Crossroads!
If you turn to the right, you will lose your horse;
To the left, your head;
If you go straight on, your life.
If you were me – which you are –
Knight at the Crossroads,
You would go home to Russia this very night.

Daddy, Daddy (1990)

Tullamore Poetry Recital

It was a one-man show in Tullamore,
'The Sonnets of Shakespeare.'
The newspaper advertisement bubbled:
'Bring Your Own Knitting.'
The audience of twenty-five
Was devout, polite, attentive,
All with their knitting,
Men and women alike with their knitting.
I shut my eyes and glimpsed
Between the tidal breakers of iambic pentameter
The knitting needles flashing like the oars of Odysseus.

But as the evening wore on, and the centuries passed,
And the meditations, and the thanksgivings,
And darkness fell, and with it a fullish moon,
Not quite full but fullish,
Putting on weight by the teaspoonful,
One was aware of a reversal advancing,
Of incoming tides being dragged backwards.
The knitting needles were no longer oars
But fiddles in orchestras sawing to halts.
One became aware of one's own silence.
One was no longer where one thought one was.
One was alone in the pit of oneself, knitting needles.

Putney Garage

to Brian Fallon

The morning after the poetry reading
At the Poetry Society in Earl's Court Square
I decided to go to a film in Leicester Square,
Having already that auburn October day
Changed my mind five times.
I would catch the 4.35 p.m. showing
Of *Au Revoir Les Enfants* in the Première.
I strolled along the north side of Piccadilly
But the closer I came to the cinema
The more I felt like going home to Brixton,
To Bill and Pippa, Ben and Sam and Jo,
In 64 Milton Road,
Pampas grass in the front garden,
Up the lane from Electric Avenue,
The child's playground that is London in October,
Its wild mildness, its puberty,
Kick of spentoutedness in my calf muscles.

I crossed over to the south side of Piccadilly,
Retraced my steps.
At the bus stop outside the Egyptian State Tourist Office
Francis Bacon was waiting for a bus;
Those ancient, glittering eyes on black steel rods
Socketed in their Sicilian pouches;
That teenager's ageing mouth
All cheek and tongue-in-cheek.

I fell into line.
We stood in silence,
He lounging against the corner of the bus shelter
In a lounge suit,
Hands in trench-coat pockets,
Belted trench coat flapping open, loose, horny epaulettes,

Black polished shoes, one over t'other,
Idly alert,
Courtly corner boy.

Luckily I had not got with me my pocket Olympus camera.
Two Number 19s passed,
Flocks of cabs.
I did not allow advertisements for the pyramids
And for a boy Pharaoh
To distract me from the nape of Bacon's neck,
The henna-dyed hairs, gelled, spiky,
Gilded in October evening sun.
The breeze lifted the hair on the crown of his skull,
The proud, soft, blown comb of the cock.

A Number 14 bus sailed into view,
The Statue of Eros in its rear-view mirror.
He put out his hand,
His left hand – bare, ungloved.
He stepped up onto the platform.
But although he was first in the queue
He stood back to permit
A young Asian gentleman,
Lean, prematurely grey,
To cut inside him to the lower deck.
Then he, aged eighty years,
Swung up the staircase like a gibbon
In the Dublin zoo.

I stepped back out of the queue,
Mulling on Vincent's memorial in Auvers
By Osip Zadkine – man at work or
Study of a man in a landscape.
I studied him sit himself down
Halfway down the aisle of the upper deck

On the north side.
What to call it? And by whom?
'Good Evening, Childhood' by J. M. W. Turner?
The bus sailed out into the smog-scrapered sun
Towards Hyde Park and Kensington,
Its terminus in white on black:
Putney Garage.

Self-Portrait, Nude with Steering Wheel

I am forty-five and do not
Know how to drive a car
– And you tell me I am cultured.

Forty-five years creeping and crawling about the earth,
Going up and down the world,
And I do not know the difference between a carburettor and a
    gasket
– And you tell me I am a Homo sapiens.

Forty-five years sitting in the back seat giving directions
– And you say that I am not an egotist.

Forty-five years sitting in the passenger seat
With my gloved hands folded primly in my lap
– And you think I am liberated.

Forty-five years getting in and out of cars
And I do not know where the dipstick is
– And you tell me that I am a superb lover.

Forty-five years grovelling behind a windscreen
– And you talk of my pride and courage and self-reliance.

Forty-five years of not caring to know the meaning of words
Like *transmission, clutch, choke, battery, leads*
– And you say that I am articulate.

Forty-five years bumming lifts off other people –
And you tell me I am an independent, solitary, romantic spirit.

So it is that you find me tonight
Loitering here outside your front door
Having paid off a taxi in three ten-pound notes,
Nude, with a steering wheel in my hands.

Sport

There were not many fields
In which you had hopes for me
But sport was one of them.
On my twenty-first birthday
I was selected to play
For Grangegorman Mental Hospital
In an away game
Against Mullingar Mental Hospital.
I was a patient
In B Wing.
You drove all the way down,
Fifty miles,
To Mullingar to stand
On the sidelines and observe me.

I was fearful I would let down
Not only my team but you.
It was Gaelic football.
I was selected as goalkeeper.
There were big country men
On the Mullingar Mental Hospital team,
Men with gapped teeth, red faces,
Oily, frizzy hair, bushy eyebrows.
Their full forward line
Were over six foot tall
Fifteen stone in weight.
All three of them, I was informed,
Cases of schizophrenia.

There was a rumour
That their centre-half forward
Was an alcoholic solicitor
Who, in a lounge bar misunderstanding,

Had castrated his best friend
But that he had no memory of it.
He had meant well – it was said.
His best friend had had to emigrate
To Nigeria.

To my surprise,
I did not flinch in the goals.
I made three or four spectacular saves,
Diving full stretch to turn
A certain goal around the corner,
Leaping high to tip another certain goal
Over the bar for a point.
It was my knowing
That you were standing on the sideline
That gave me the necessary motivation –
That will to die
That is as essential to sportsmen as to artists.
More than anybody it was you
I wanted to mesmerise, and after the game –
Grangegorman Mental Hospital
Having defeated Mullingar Mental Hospital
By 14 goals and 38 points to 3 goals and 10 points –
Sniffing your approval, you shook hands with me.
'Well played, son.'

I may not have been mesmeric
But I had not been mediocre.
In your eyes I had achieved something at last.
On my twenty-first birthday I had played on a winning team
The Grangegorman Mental Hospital team.
Seldom if ever again in your eyes
Was I to rise to these heights.

Apartheid

When after twenty-seven sessions of Electric Convulsive Therapy
I was discharged from hospital in London,
I got the night train from Euston to Holyhead,
Sipping baby gin-and-tonics in my empty carriage,
Savouring the consolation of the passing night,
The invisible emptiness of the universe.
Daddy and Mummy met me at seven-thirty next morning
Off the boat train at Westland Row.

Driving home through the deserted streets of Dublin,
None of us could think of anything to say
Until outside the National Maternity Hospital
Daddy imparted to me that in the afternoon
He and I would be attending the Rugby International
Between Ireland and South Africa.
Our cousin, it seemed, was playing in the front row
Of the scrum for Ireland,
Propping up the scrum for Ireland.

As I sit in the East Stand freezing,
All the men of Ireland with rugs on their laps,
Whiskey flasks in their hip pockets,
I ask Daddy why there are no black men
On the African team.
'Apartheid' – he answers authoritatively – 'Apartheid.'
He pronounces the word *Apartheid*
With such élan, such expertise,
With such familiarity, such finality,
As if it were a part of nature,
Part of ourselves.

I try to remember what Apartheid is.
I cannot remember what Apartheid is.
Odd to think that only this day last week in London

I was having my twenty-seventh session of Electric Convulsive
    Therapy
While today I am sitting in the East Stand in Dublin
Watching an African team with no black men
Playing an Irish team with all white men,
Daddy's arm around me, his chin jutting out.
If I was a black man, I would play for Africa.

Glocca Morra

Dear Daughter – Watching my father die,
As one day you will watch me die,
In the public ward of a centre-city hospital,
Mid-afternoon bustle,
A transistor radio playing two or three beds away,
Paintwork flaking on the wall,
His breath dwindling,
His throat gurgling,
A source disappearing,
Source of all that I am before my eyes disappearing,
Well, watching your own father die slowly in front of you,
Die slowly right under your nose,
Is a bit like sitting in the front row of the concert hall
Watching a maestro performing Tchaikovsky's Grand Piano Sonata.
It's spectacular, so to speak,
But the audience feels helpless.

When Daddy died
I wrung my hands at the foot of his bed
Until a consultant doctor told me to stop it
And to show some respect for the dead.
The old prick.
He had done nothing for Daddy
Except pollute him with pills for twenty years
For fees in guineas.
They threw a sheet over him
And put screens around his bed
But I stood my ground
At the foot of the bed
While the transistor radio,
Like something hidden in a hedgerow,

Went on with its programme –
Rosemary Clooney crooning
'How are Things in Glocca Morra?'

Outside the ward window –
Which was in need of cleaning, I noticed –
The sun was going down in the west over the Phoenix Park
Where Daddy and me
('Daddy and I' – he corrects me –
He was a stickler for grammar),
Where Daddy and I
Played all sorts of games for years,
Football, hurling, cricket, golf, donkey,
Before he got into his Abraham-and-Isaac phase
And I got the boat to England
Before he had time to chop off my head.

O Daddy dear –
As we find ourselves alone together for the last time,
Marooned in this centre-city hospital public ward,
I think that there is something consoling – cheerful, even –
About that transistor playing away in the next bed.
The day you bought your first transistor
You took us out for a drive in the car,
The Vauxhall Viva,
Down to a derelict hotel by the sea,
The Glocca Morra,
Roofless, windowless, silent,
And, you used add with a chuckle,
Scandalous.
You dandled it on your knee
And you stated how marvellous a gadget it was,
A portable transistor,
And that you did not have to pay
A licence fee for it,

You chuckled.
A man not much known for chuckling.
The Glocca Morra,
Roofless, windowless, silent and *scandalous*.

Rosemary Clooney –
The tears are lumbering down my cheeks, Dad –
She must be about the same age as you,
Even looks like you.
I bet her handwriting
Is much the same as yours,
You had a lovely hand,
Cursive, flourishing, exuberant, actual.
Whatever things are like in Glocca Morra
I'm sad that we're not going to be together any more.
Dear Daughter – When the time comes
For you to watch me die,
In a public place to watch me
Trickling away from you,
Consider the paintwork on the wall
And check out the music in the next bed.
'How are Things in Glocca Morra?'
Every bit as bad as you might think they are –
Or as good. Or not so bad. Love, Dad.

Crazy About Women (1991)

Flower Girl, Dublin

after Jack B. Yeats

Afternoons in winter
I sit in Robert Roberts' café
Watching men and women,
Especially women.
I am crazy about women.

Just because I am a man without a woman
Does not mean that I have no interest in women.
In fact, I am preoccupied with fundamentally nothing else.
I read all of Nietzsche when I was seventeen.
Then it was time to grow up.

Would you please hose some of your hot liquid into me?
Mother of five to boy at coffee dispenser.
She must be forty at least but as she sips her grounds –
Her Costa Rican grounds –
As she smacks her lips
Trickling her tongue tip along her lip rim
She is a girl not yet nineteen
Haughty as an Englishwoman in Shanghai.
Red cloche hat, grey wool overcoat,
Black low high-heel shoes.

I see in today's newspaper a black-and-white photograph
Of a woman in a black miniskirt at the opening
Of the Sean McSweeney retrospective last night
(There is a man who can paint – not many can
Since the Great Yeat died in 1957).

But much as that photo causes a stir in me –
An abstract stir in me –
It is as nothing compared to this glimpse of ankle –
Ankle –

Of the mother of five in red cloche hat –
Would you please hose some of your hot liquid into me?

Time to go – home. I dally to loiter
In the doorway of the café eyeing myself
In the shop window opposite, my bowler hat,
My frock coat, my gleaming galoshes.
A flower girl with a single red rose in her hands
Is passing the time of day with the mother of five
Not making any particular pitch to sell.

Timorousness entices me to my right –
But I know, Jack, I know
I should step briskly to my left,
Proffer the single red rose to the mother of five,
Nail my colours to the mast.
Will I or won't I?
And give all my loose change to the flower girl –
All my loose change?

A Snail in My Prime (1993)

Father's Day, 21 June 1992

Just as I was dashing to catch the Dublin–Cork train,
Dashing up and down the stairs, searching my pockets,
She told me that her sister in Cork wanted a loan of the axe;
It was late June and
The buddleia tree in the backyard
Had grown out of control.
The taxi was ticking over outside in the street,
All the neighbours noticing it.
'You mean that you want me to bring her down the axe?'
'Yes, if you wouldn't mind, that is –'
'A simple saw would do the job, surely to God
She could borrow a simple saw.'
'She said that she'd like the axe.'
'OK. There is a Blue Cabs taxi ticking over outside
And the whole world inspecting it,
I'll bring her down the axe.'
The axe – all four-and-a-half feet of it –
Was leaning up against the wall behind the settee –
The fold-up settee that doubles as a bed.
She handed the axe to me just as it was,
As neat as a newborn babe,
All in the bare buff.
You'd think she'd have swaddled it up
In something – if not a blanket, an old newspaper,
But no, not even a token hanky
Tied in a bow round its head.
I decided not to argue the toss. I kissed her goodbye.

The whole long way down to Cork
I felt uneasy. Guilt feelings.
It's a killer, this guilt.
I always feel bad leaving her
But this time it was the worst.

I could see that she was glad
To see me go away for a while,
Glad at the prospect of being
Two weeks on her own,
Two weeks of having the bed to herself,
Two weeks of not having to be pestered
By my coarse advances,
Two weeks of not having to look up from her plate
And behold me eating spaghetti with a knife and fork.
Our daughters are all grown up and gone away.
Once when she was sitting pregnant on the settee
It snapped shut with herself inside it,
But not a bother on her. I nearly died.

As the train slowed down approaching Portarlington
I overheard myself say to the passenger sitting opposite me:
'I am feeling guilty because she does not love me
As much as she used to, can you explain that?'
The passenger's eyes were on the axe on the seat beside me.
'Her sister wants a loan of the axe . . .'
As the train threaded itself into Portarlington
I nodded to the passenger 'Cúl an tSúdaire!'
The passenger stood up, lifted down a case from the rack,
Walked out of the coach, but did not get off the train.
For the remainder of the journey, we sat alone,
The axe and I,
All the green fields running away from us,
All our daughters grown up and gone away.

A Cold Wind Blew in from Lake Geneva

Belovèd daughters, I would like to be cremated
Early in the afternoon, 3.30 p.m. at the latest;
A woman to say Psalm 23;
A painter to say a poem from memory;
A poet to hold up a painting;
An architect to improvise a slow air.

Throw a party –
The kind of party that Michael Cullen
Threw in Brighton Vale in April '92,
Or in Henrietta Street in April '90:
A stand-up feast, a round table piled,
Bread and wine, the best of cheeses,
Homemade pâté, olives, cucumbers,
Salami, hams, salads,
Strawberries, pineapples, melons, cream,
Bouquets of irises, daffodils, chrysanthemums,
The window open to the street.
Open all windows, let breezes
Catch napes, necks, breasts,
Cheekbones, earlobes, curtains.
When the poet Rilke died
Someone at that instant opened the bedroom window
And a cold wind blew in from Lake Geneva.

Invite by advertisement,
By word of mouth,
Anyone who felt the slightest
Affection for the deceased.
In my name drink a toast
To Human Nature and Frailty.
Whisper my two logos: *Provincials to the Wall*
And – *Never Conform.*

Later, when it suits –
When you have a weekend to spare –
Take back my ashes to Mayo,
Climb the Reek on a blue day,
Scatter my ashes in the direction of Clew Bay.
Not to worry if a west wind
Blows them back in the opposite direction –
That would be in the nature of things.

If all that is asking too much
Take my ashes out for a walk in Ringsend
Down the Drain;
No more seductive entrance to the world
Than the Drain in Ringsend;
Not even the Champs-Elysées
Quite match the Drain;
Down Pigeon House Road,
Past the Tech,
Past the Toll Bridge,
Down to the Gut;
No more seductive exit from the world
Than the Gut in Ringsend;
Not even the Statue of Liberty
Quite matches the Gut.

Cast me out into the Gut
So that one will never know exactly
Whether my ashes fetched up
In Dodder or Liffey or Grand Canal:
The thing in the end being The Mixture.
PS
If you would rather not,
I mean if all of this strikes you as too, too much,

Put my ashes in a black refuse sack and remember
To put it out on Wednesday morning
Along with the dustbin and the empties –
The golden, golden empties.

Give Me Your Hand (1994)

The Arnolfini Marriage

after Jan van Eyck

We are the Arnolfinis.
Do not think you may invade
Our privacy because you may not.

We are standing to our portrait,
The most erotic portrait ever made,
Because we have faith in the artist

To do justice to the plurality,
Fertility, domesticity, barefootedness
Of a man and a woman saying 'we':

To do justice to our bed
As being our most necessary furniture;
To do justice to our life as a reflection.

Our brains spill out upon the floor
And the terrier at our feet sniffs
The minutiae of our magnitude.

The most relaxing word in our vocabulary is 'we'.
Imagine being able to say 'we'.
Most people are in no position to say 'we'.

Are you? Who eat alone? Sleep alone?
And at dawn cycle to work
With an Alsatian shepherd dog tied to your handlebars?

We will pause now for the Angelus.
Here you have it:
The two halves of the coconut.

Christmas Day (1996)

from Christmas Day

[. . .]

The skin on my face
Is beige and my hair is grey
From woman-hunger.
For days the phone
Does not ring and then
When it does and I run
To snatch it up
The shy, reticent voice
Of a woman in the South Island,
New Zealand, whispers
'I'd like to knit you a woolly hat
But I don't know
What is between those ears of yours.'
To live alone
Is not to know
One day from the next:
Letting myself in
And out of the house;
Tramping the streets
With my skull on my neck
And with my hand in my pocket
Twiddling my house key.
Christmas is the Feast of St Loneliness.
I streetwalk at night
Looking in the windows
Of other people's houses
Assessing their Christmas decorations,
Marking them out of ten.
This Christmas I have spotted
In the front window of a three-storey
Town house in Percy Place
A little Christmas tree
Adorned only

With electric candles.
I give it eight out of ten.
What amazes me this Christmas
Is all the menorahs.
Menorahs are all the craze.
Every second window in Ringsend
Has a menorah. Oh, Sharon,
Your menorah is only gorgeous.
Don't be talking, Deborah.

[. . .]

He invited me out of the blue
A week ago
The day I drove him down
In the snow
To visit his mother in Jericho –
A hospice where old people
Subsist with a soupçon of dignity
As they queue up for the final curtain,
An oasis in the desert.
Over the hills
And far away
In County Wicklow.
How many curtains to Jericho?

[. . .]

Frank is in the kitchen
Cooking Christmas Dinner
For himself and myself.
He and I for Christmas Dinner.
'Are you in good voice, Paul?
Your speaking-in-public-voice?
Chant me a new anthem.'

124

I demur but Frank insists.
I chant him a new anthem –
'An Item Once Again':

> *An item once again!*
> *An item once again!*
> *If you promise me you'll laugh all day,*
> *You can have me for your birthday.*

[. . .]

It is five in the afternoon.
He switches off the television.
We listen – at my instigation –
To a fifteen-minute programme on the wireless
Advertised in the *Guide*
As the true story behind Robert Frost's poem
'Stopping by Woods on a Snowy Evening'.
We raise our eyebrows, purse our lips,
Shake our heads. No, sir, no.
The poem is the true story.
The true story is a lie.
Did it really happen?
If it was fictional, it happened.
Only the fictional is real.
Only the silken
Tent is real.
Only the bumble bee.
'At your instigation, Paul.'
'At my instigation, Frank.'
'And miles to go before I sleep . . .'
We yawn. We look at our watches.
'Frank, do you believe in the Annunciation?'
'I do, Paul, do you?'
'I do, Frank, and the sensational thing about it –

And I have only begun to realize this
Since receiving from Father Pat O'Brien of Skehanna
A haiku poem of his own making for Christmas
In which Mary says to the Angel Gabriel
Yes I will Yes I will yes yes yes –
For Christ's sake, Frank, the Annunciation
Is the ultimate yes-saying to life.
Mary leaves Molly Bloom sitting up in bed.'

    [. . .]

Greetings to Our Friends
in Brazil (1999)

Island Musician Going Home

after Veronica Bolay

Driving home alone the bog road at night in the rain
Leaving the village behind me, its harbour lights
Pegging down the marquee of the sea,
I am half sunk by the stone of my heart.

Mile after mile of bog road in the night in the rain,
Not a single dwelling on the mountain either side of the road,
Not knowing when a mountain sheep will light up under my
    wheels,
My audience all couples canoodling behind in the village.

But when I drive up to the maroon-painted five-barred gate
And I switch off my lights, and I climb out of my car,
And I can see nothing, and I can hear nothing,
I see again that home is the skirl of silence.

I kiss the darkness, and all loneliness abandons me.
A life without a wife is nothing to boast about
But that's music. I walk back up the road
Kissing the darkness; and a small mouth of cold gold

In the clouds is becoming aware of its soul.

Waterloo Road

On Waterloo Road on an August day
I met Patrick Kavanagh in his garden flat.
After I rang the bell there was a long pause –
To open . . . or not to open –
Before I identified two sad, wise, humourous eyes
In black horn
Peering out at me through the spyhole window high up in
    the door.

Patrick Kavanagh led me up the long hall
To the living room at the back looking out on the garden.
He sat down in an ocean-going armchair of a past era
With dozens of anthologies of American poetry
In stacks round about his shoeless feet on the floor.
He blinked up into the skies behind me:
'The American anthology is great for the kickstart.'
We sat in silence – two deferential elephants.
He the old cobbler at the term of his days;
I the young apprentice in my first pregnancy.
'The apprenticeship,' he declared eagerly, sitting out forward
'The apprenticeship, you know, is twenty years.'

It was a golden day on Waterloo Road –
Blue skies, shirt sleeves, bicycles, miniskirts –
As we strolled down to the Waterloo House
Past Michael Kane's big window for a lunchtime drink.
There was an anticyclone over Ireland.
At the construction site on the corner of Waterloo Road
That was to become the office block of the Yellow Pages
Patrick Kavanagh halted with his hands on his hips
Gazing up at the meteoric men in yellow hats
Walking tightropes smoking fags.
From them to me he switched gaze solemnly.

Divining the mystery of the universe, he announced:
'Men at Work!' He tossed his head back. 'Men at Work!'

That day Patrick Kavanagh had a wedding to go to
In the Shangri-La Hotel on the hill of Dalkey.
Through the armies of the sun we rode a taxi
Like Lenny Bruce and Billy the Kid
In a chariot along the shore of Dublin Bay.
Although I was homeless, jobless, futureless,
I felt wholly safe in Patrick Kavanagh's company.
I uttered: 'Today is such a golden day
It reminds me of days I stayed in the monastery –
The Trappist Monastery at Mount Melleray.'

Consternation in the back of the taxi.
Patrick Kavanagh groaned:
'On a summer's day like today
Don't be thinking about monasteries.
On a summer's day like today
You should be thinking about beautiful women.'
When in the lobby of the Shangri-La
The head waiter spotted us
He took us for a pair of winos,
Made to throw us out,
Only for the bridegroom to rescue us.
Patrick Kavanagh was the guest of honour.

Humming snatches of 'On Raglan Road'
Patrick Kavanagh sat down on a couch behind me –
'For that I'll vouch on any couch' –
While I, sitting up at the bar, found
Myself beside a beautiful woman
With long red hair, green eyes, freckles.
Nessa O'Neill was her name and she invited me

To go for a swim with her at the bottom of the garden.
The Shangri-La backed on to the Irish Sea.

There was an Indian Summer that year in Ireland
And in October she and I set up home in London.
We lived together sixteen years,
Rearing two golden girls.

On Waterloo Road on the first of August I met her first and knew
That her red hair would weave a snare that I would never rue;
I embraced the danger, I sailed along in the enchanted cab
And I rowed my oar by the star of Patrick Kavanagh.

Cries of an Irish Caveman (2001)

from Give Him Bondi

[. . .]

Pounding forwards I am surging backwards.
Instead of me catching the waves,
The waves are dumping me backwards!
I who presume myself a porpoise
With fifty years of Floating Theory
Chalked up on my flippers
Am now a mouse being toyed with
By the tom-cat of the sea!
In this drifting micromoment
The stopwatch stops:
I behold my death eyeball me
Like a sadistic schoolmaster
Cornering me at the blackboard.

I wave, but no one sees me
And, as I wave, I begin to sink.
I'm being eaten alive.
Save me, O Christ, save me!
Your what? Your own death?
Your own end? Your own oblivion?
Death by drowning?
        The fury of it!
The remorseless deep closing o'er your head!
Alone, alone, all, all alone!
Within seconds, to be but a swab –
A trace in water –
That scarcely decipherable but tell-tale trace
In the sea after a substance has sunk.
Fear frying your bones.
I thought I had known fear –
Oceans of fear – but I had not:
Not until now
This micromoment of 100-carat fear;

My body incapable of coping
But my psyche clear with fear
Not muddled or mesmerised,
But clarifed – a seer
Of the final second, seeing
The sea about to snatch,
Suck, swallow me.

The sea! Oh, the sea!
That stunning, wholly together She –
The one with her Mountain Passes
In all the right places.
You've flirted with her all your life
Having it both ways as always;
Your wife your mistress not your wife;
Your mistress your wife not your mistress;
Solitude your company;
Being mortal claiming immortality;
Every single time without exception
That the air hostess models the life jacket
You insouciantly ignore her,
Flaunting yourself a superior stoic
Who plumbs the secret of the voyage.
Voyager your voyage about to end
Faster than an airliner plummeting
How goes your voyaging?

Why are you standing in water
Out of your depth dying?
Far from your own bed?
Naught now between your legs
But disdainful water?
Being buried alive?
Dying, Durcan, dying
In your own standing?

Hanging on by one hand
From the sky's yardarm
About to plop
Down into Davy Jones's locker?
Where be your swashbuckling now?
Your hip-hop-hip mating?
Your waistcoated machismo?
Where be all your cheek-to-cheek glowing?
Your eyebrow-to-eyebrow acrobatics?
Where be all your toe-to-toe conniving?
You are being struck down,
Having glowed, having connived.
Neither being seen nor being heard
But tomorrow in a scrap of newscasting
On ABC:
'Irish poet trapped in rips,
Washed up between the Heads
Of Sydney Harbour.'

Ocean – compleat ocean – clenches me
In its JCB claws,
Hissing at me that this time there'll be no pause
And my brains gape down upon my own terror.
In the vice of drowning I know
I have no power, my fate
Decided, all I can
Be said to be doing is lingering;
Out of my depth, flailing
Legs, arms, caterwauling
In my kitty
And meekly screaming – I am lingering;
Fresh blows the breeze from off the bow;
My Irish boy, where lingerest thou?
This fling in which you're lingering
Will last but seconds and after

You will be but a thing
Flung against the automatic sliding doors
Of the sea's casino.
My father and mother
Each a wowser
Resenting one another,
Resented me
Because I was a bother.
How so much better
It would have been
Not to have given birth
To such a bother.
All presumption walloped o'er the horizon,
All my naïveté, all my toxic pride,
All my vanity, all my conceit.
There is nothing I can do – I realise –
Except shout, bawl, cry, whimper.
In the cot of the sea,
On the rails of the waves
I bang my little knuckles.
The sea seethes:
Paul Durcan, you are
The epitome of futility.

I cry out 'Help! Help!'
But no one hears me.
A cry? I –
Did I ever reply
To a cry?
A cry of a tiny, frail Scotsman
In a damp basement bedsit
In Buckingham Palace Road
Choking on his own loneliness?
Aye! A cry!
Nobody hears me, the dead man!

I cry out again with all my ego.
The about-to-be-overtaken sprinter
At the finishing line,
Lunging one last futile fingertipslength.
The ocean is the mighty woman
You have hunted all your life.
But now that she has got you
In the palm of her hand –
In her thimble of no reprieve! –
You are crying out 'Help!'
She is moulding her knuckles around you.
You are her prey.
This is the yarn you will not live to spin,
The blackest yarn,
A groundswell is spinning out your life
At once slowly, speedily –
A groundswell no longer a cliché
But a mother of death!
You are a puppet out of your depth
And your legs are diced dancers
Dangling from deadwood,
Thrashing in their throes
Out of sight slipping.
The sea is a headless goddess
All flesh sans eyes sans mouth.
Paul Durcan, this is one lady
Through whose eyes and mouth,
Through whose free looks
You will not talk your way.

HELP!
My teensy-weensy voicette fetches
Over the uncut surf and the sealed ocean
To two young men who shout back –
Their seal heads bobbing a quarter-mile off –

Something like 'Hold on! Hold on!'
And blubbering I pant for breath
As my head slides beneath the waves,
My shoulders caving in,
My paunch of guts dragging me down,
My kidneys wincing,
My crimson ankles skipping,
My snow-white fetlocks like faulty pistons
Halting for the last time.

I can hear myself sobbing 'O God, O God!'
Floating downwards with every surge;
Hurtling upwards with every heave.
'O Christ, I don't want to die!
After all that church-going and hymn-singing
This is not the only life I know
But it's the only life I want!
I WANT TO LIVE!'
They clutch me round the neck
And flail and thrash to lug me shorewards.
A third joins them – an off-duty lifeguard
Called Brian who happens to be doing
A stint of training – but the breaking rollers
At each crash uppercut me.
Each other roller clubs me on the head.
Not once of course, but again again
Clubbing, clubbing, clubbing,
Such stuffing as is in me goes limp.
My rescuers scream: 'Keep your lips tight shut!'
As each wave crashes I writhe for consciousness –
A newborn baby pawing air;
My lungs spewing up bladders of salt water –
The rash smart sloggering brine.
Wrenching me they fling me shorewards –
These three fierce young men –

Until they lash me to a surfboard
And sail me in facedown the final furlong,
The final rumble strips of foam,
Racing the shoreline, beaching me,
Dumping me on wet sand bereft of ocean,
Raising me up by the armpits, hauling me.
On my hands and knees
In amber froth
I crawl the final metre.
On the keel of an upturned boat I sat down
And wept and shivered and stretched to vomit.
Sat retching there like a shredded parsnip,
The cowering genius of the shore.
Another Bondi casualty bent forlorn
Upon the tourist shingles
Of New South Wales.

[. . .]

Homage to Tracey Emin

I

Apart from being a unique work of art
What appals me about Tracey Emin's bedroom
Is how similar it is to my own bedroom –
Same white sheets the colour of stagnant dishwater –
Same worndown, wornout, scruffy slippers,
Punched out pill sachets, underwear, price tags –
U-W Bra White 32C £31.00 –
One unopened bottle of *Orangina*
And in blue neon in the ceiling
The legend as in my own bedroom
Every Part Of Me's Bleeding
And I drink much of the night
And I stay in bed in the morning.

Tracey Emin is a seaside of fresh air.
Tracey Emin is the T. S. Eliot *de nos jours.*
Tracey Emin on Margate Sands
        can connect nothing with nothing.
Inside every fluid human
A small girl is frozen
In the wings waiting to walk on
To ask the sixty-thousand dollar question
At the Cardinal's Ball:
Where does the holy water come from?

II

That autumn the winds came and blew the leaves off
    the trees
And there were leaves stuck to the windscreens of the cars
And I saw that the lines on my face were pleasant places
And I took the first flight out of Gatwick
To go find my father on the shores of Cyprus.

Father, will you swim with me in the high seas?
Will we jump together?

Tracey, Tracey, hold on tight

7 December 1999

Torn in Two

That twenty-two page love letter in which
I slopped out my heart to you,
Comparing you, my mountain woman,
With a gold hoard secreted in loughwater
Under a thorn tree in Rear Cross –
How I waited day after day for a reply,
Week after week, month after month.
When after seven months a reply came
I did not recognise your hand on the envelope
But inside there it was, my letter,
My twenty-two page love letter, all of it,
Which you had torn in two.

I am a bright man torn in two.
Have I no hope of being a union with you?
Not a eunuch – a union?
I get up every day torn in two.
I trudge over to the minimart torn in two.
I buy my sliced pan torn in two.
I buy my low-fat milk torn in two.
I traipse back home torn in two.
I crouch in front of the TV torn in two.
I gobble my microwave dinner torn in two.
I kneel down at my bed torn in two.
I whisper my bedtime prayers torn in two.
I clamber into bed torn in two.
But I cannot go to sleep torn in two.
I read about the Taliban torn in two.
I spend the night on my back torn in two.
I get up every day torn in two.
Have I no hope of being one with you?
I am a bright man torn in two.

The Art of Life (2004)

The Man with a Bit of Jizz in Him

My husband is a man –
With a bit of jizz in him.
On Monday night in Sligo I said to him:
'Let's go someplace for a week
Before the winter is on top of us.'
He said: 'Where would you like to go?'
I said: 'Down south – West Cork or Kerry.'
He said: 'Too much hassle.'
I said: 'Where would you like to go?'
He said: 'Dublin Airport early tomorrow morning.
I'll drive halfway, you drive halfway.'
We caught the Aer Lingus Dublin-Nice direct flight:
180 euro return.
Driving to Dublin he phoned his niece in Hertz.
He said: 'I want a car in Nice.'
Hertz gave us a brand-new Peugeot.
Only thirty miles on the clock.
(If you're over forty-five, they give you a big car.
If you're a young fellow, they give you a small car
That you can go and crash.)
There's only two ways out of Nice Airport –
West or East: simple.
At the first filling station he stopped
And asked the way to St-Paul-de-Vence.
'St-Paul-de-Vence? Exit 48
And do not come on to the motorway again
Until you want to go back to Ireland.'
An hour later I was lying on a duvet
In a three-star hotel in St-Paul-de-Vence.
It was spotless. Spotless!
I was that pleased with him I shook his hand
And pulled him in under the duvet with me.
An attractive middle-aged housewife I may be *but* –
There is nothing to beat a man with a bit of jizz in him.

Achill Island Man

On Achill Island when I wake in the morning
I find myself in the Amusements Arcade of my own body
And I am standing up against the pinball machine
And I insert 20 cents and I give it a kick
And I watch all the small pink balls of pain
Tripping on lights all over my body.
Oh! No!
Toes! Knees! Elbows! Shoulder-blades!
Everywhere I look, small pink balls of pain
And I mind not to rub my neck. Anyways,
I come out of the arcade and I blink
And, despite all the weather
In my body every place I look,
I do have to smile at all those lights
Going on and off. It's amazing, I think,
It's amazing I'm still alive. Oh, man!
No, I never watch television!
I might have colon cancer. I might not.
I might have lumbago or sciatica.
I might have gallstones. I might have ulcers.
I might have diverticulitis!
I might have auricular fibrillation!
I might have diabetes!
As a matter of fact, I do have diabetes,
But with the pills it's all the one.
Will I bother having a haircut?
I will bother having a haircut
And I will get a lift home
In time for the five o'clock removal of my neighbour
Who was seventy-one – she had a year on me –
And who was a very quiet woman, but as good a woman
        as you'd find in all of Achill Island

And after that I will have three pints in The Crossroads Inn –
Maybe four –
And after that I will go home and have my dinner
And after dinner I will go to bed and begin
The whole story all over again – isn't that it?

Ireland 2002

Do you ever take a holiday abroad?
No, we always go to America.

The 2003 World Snooker Championship

Don't lecture me about lint on the baize –
I am ninety-six years of age.

What an old woman like me needs
More than a meal or medicine
Or a life sentence in a nursing home
Is seventeen days in front of the television
In my own home
Watching the World Snooker Championship
In the Crucible in Sheffield.
Although I like rugby,
I am a snooker fanatic.

Don't lecture me about lint on the baize –
I am ninety-six years of age.

I am frail and cranky
And I have a pain in my neck
That would make Humpty Dumpty
Grateful to fall off his wall,
But at a crucial moment in the Crucible
I sizzle with satisfaction
At the spectacle of a young man's bottom
As he bends down low over the green baize
To pot the black –
A superbly turned-out young man's trim bottom,
The left cheek of which is streamlined
With shoe heel and collar bone
When he lifts his left leg to spread-eagle it
Like a pedigree cocker spaniel
Along the kerb of the table.

Don't lecture me about lint on the baize –
I am ninety-six years of age.

And when that young man hails
From Ranelagh, Dublin 6,
And when his name is Ken
I am as much a believer in the Resurrection
As the Pope in Rome.
If there is a heaven –
One must not say so
But I doubt it –
Heaven would be the Triangle at night
Of snooker tables lit by floodlights
Under the whites of whose eyes
Thousands upon thousands upon thousands
Of trim-bottomed young men
Would be chalking their cues
Before focussing their perfect pelvises
On the white cue ball,
The red and the black,
And on all the coloured balls –
All the coloured balls.

Don't lecture me about lint on the baize –
I am ninety-six years of age.

Rosie Joyce

I

That was that Sunday afternoon in May
When a hot sun pushed through the clouds
And you were born!

I was driving the two hundred miles from west to east,
The sky blue-and-white china in the fields
In impromptu picnics of tartan rugs;

When neither words nor I
Could have known that you had been named already
And that your name was Rosie –

Rosie Joyce! May you some day in May
Fifty-six years from today be as lucky
As I was when you were born that Sunday:

To drive such side-roads, such main roads, such ramps, such
        roundabouts,
To cross such bridges, to by-pass such villages, such towns
As I did on your Incarnation Day.

By-passing Swinford – Croagh Patrick in my rear-view mirror –
My mobile phone rang and, stopping on the hard edge of
        P. Flynn's highway,
I heard Mark your father say:

'A baby girl was born at 3.33 p.m.
Weighing 7 and a 1/2 lbs in Holles Street.
Tough work, all well.'

153

II

That Sunday in May before daybreak
Night had pushed up through the slopes of Achill
Yellow forefingers of Arum Lily – the first of the year;

Down at the Sound the first rhododendrons
Purpling the golden camps of whins;
The first hawthorns powdering white the mainland;

The first yellow irises flagging roadside streams;
Quills of bog-cotton skimming the bogs;
Burrishoole cemetery shin-deep in forget-me-nots;

The first sea pinks speckling the seashore;
Cliffs of London Pride, groves of bluebell,
First fuchsia, Queen Anne's Lace, primrose.

I drove the Old Turlough Road, past Walter Durcan's Farm,
Umbrella'd in the joined handwriting of its ash trees;
I drove Tulsk, Kilmainham, the Grand Canal.

Never before had I felt so fortunate
To be driving back into Dublin city;
Each canal bridge an old pewter brooch.

I rode the waters and the roads of Ireland,
Rosie, to be with you, seashell at my ear!
How I laughed when I cradled you in my hand.

Only at Tarmonbarry did I slow down,
As in my father's Ford Anglia half a century ago
He slowed down also, as across the River Shannon

We crashed, rattled and bounced on a Bailey bridge;
Daddy relishing his role as Moses,
Enunciating the name of the Great Divide

Between the East and the West!
We are the people of the West,
Our fate to go East.

No such thing, Rosie, as a Uniform Ireland
And please God there never will be;
There is only the River Shannon and all her sister rivers

And all her brother mountains and their family prospects.
There are higher powers than politics
And these we call wildflowers or, geologically, people.

Rosie Joyce – that Sunday in May
Not alone did you make my day, my week, my year
To the prescription of Jonathan Philbin Bowman –

Daymaker!
Daymaker!
Daymaker!

Popping out of my daughter, your mother –
Changing the expressions on the faces all around you –
All of them looking like blue hills in a heat haze –

But you saved my life. For three years
I had been subsisting in the slums of despair,
Unable to distinguish one day from the next.

III

On the return journey from Dublin to Mayo
In Charlestown on Main Street
I meet John Normanly, organic farmer from Curry.

He is driving home to his wife Caroline
From a Mountbellew meeting of the Western Development
    Commission
Of Dillon House in Ballaghaderreen.

He crouches in his car, I waver in the street,
As we exchange lullabies of expectancy;
We wet our foreheads in John Moriarty's autobiography.

The following Sunday is the Feast of the Ascension
Of Our Lord into Heaven:
Thank You, O Lord, for the Descent of Rosie onto Earth.

The Laughter of Mothers (2007)

A View of the Bridge

I was standing at the window of my shoe shop at
    eleven o'clock in the morning
Admiring the baskets of flowers on the lamp-posts that
    we'd hung up the previous week
And wondering if I'd bother buying a national
    newspaper across the river in McGreevy's –
What's the point in buying a national newspaper?
    Maybe I should be thinking
About buying a copy of the *International Herald Tribune*
    if it's in –
When who do I see coming over the bridge, the
    three-arched bridge in the centre of our town,
But Seamus Heaney and John McGahern, our two
    world-famous authors, strolling slowly,
Strolling *very* slowly, fresh as daisies, arm in arm at
    eleven o'clock in the morning.
Fresh as daisies, yet men of an older vintage than me.
I couldn't believe it. It was about four years ago. I ran
    back into the shop
And fetched out the great ledger that we've had for a
    hundred-and-two years and a fountain pen
And I went to rush out the door only for my guardian
    angel to grab me by the scruff of the neck.
'Woa boy, woa, boy, woa, woa!' my guardian angel
    neighed into my ear
As I gawked out the door at the two world-famous
    authors as they stood
At the end of the bridge on my side of the river
    glancing over at my shoe shop –
Or seeming to, for they were totally engrossed in their
    conversation.
They looked like two sheep farmers after coming out
    of Sunday Mass,

In their Sunday half-best, black slacks, black slip-ons,
       tweed jackets, open-neck white shirts,
Not so much striking a bargain between themselves as
       discussing
A grander bargain having been struck somewhere else
       that they had witnessed.
For the love of God, I muttered to myself, it's not
       every day or every week
Or every year or every hundred years that you'd see
       two world-famous authors
Walking the streets of a small town in the west of
       Ireland and yet –
What right have I to interrupt their morning, their
       morning stroll,
Their conversation, their sacred conversation? 'Holy God,'
I roared at myself, 'but you have no right to do such a
       thing!'
I put down the great ledger of 1903 on the counter
And folded my arms and crossed my legs and
       immediately
I felt an indescribable surge of surprise and good
       fortune and common sense
As I watched them turn around under a high basket of
       fresh flowers and walk off down along the river into
       the trees.
In our small town we may be behind the times in lots
       of ways, but we're no huxters like some I won't
       name in big cities not far away, isn't life gas?

The MacBride Dynasty

What young mother is not a vengeful goddess
Spitting dynastic as well as motherly pride?
In 1949 in the black Ford Anglia,
Now that I had become a walking, talking little boy,
Mummy drove me out to visit my grand-aunt Maud
     Gonne
In Roebuck House in the countryside near Dublin,
To show off to the servant of the Queen
The latest addition to the extended family.
Although the eighty-year-old Cathleen Ni Houlihan
     had taken to her bed
She was keen as ever to receive admirers,
Especially the children of the family.
Only the previous week the actor MacLiammóir
Had been kneeling at her bedside reciting Yeats to her,
His hand on his heart, clutching a red rose.
Cousin Seán and his wife Kid led the way up the
     stairs,
Seán opening the door and announcing my mother.
Mummy lifted me up in her arms as she approached
     the bed
And Maud leaned forward, sticking out her claws
To embrace me, her lizards of eyes darting about
In the rubble of the ruins of her beautiful face.
Terrified, I recoiled from her embrace
And, fleeing her bedroom, ran down the stairs
Out onto the wrought-iron balcony
Until Seán caught up with me and quieted me
And took me for a walk in the walled orchard.
Mummy was a little but not totally mortified:
She had never liked Maud Gonne because of Maud's
Betrayal of her husband, Mummy's Uncle John,
Major John, most ordinary of men, most

Humorous, courageous of soldiers,
The pride of our family,
Whose memory always brought laughter
To my grandmother Eileen's lips. 'John,'
She used cry, 'John was such a gay man.'
Mummy set great store by loyalty; loyalty
In Mummy's eyes was the cardinal virtue.
Maud Gonne was a disloyal wife
And, therefore, not worthy of Mummy's love.
For dynastic reasons we would tolerate Maud,
But we would always see through her.

Treasure Island

On his sixth birthday, October 16th, 1950,
His mother took him to see his first film.
If she had promised him only a bus ride
Into the city centre
He would have been frantic with expectation,
But not only did she take him on a bus ride
Into the city centre – the Number 11
Into Nelson's Pillar, just she and he alone
In the front seat together on the upstairs deck –
But on disembarking in O'Connell Street
She took him by the hand and steered him
Up the steps of the Metropole Cinema.
This new, until-now forbidden world of cinema
Was a second extension of his mother's bedroom
(The first extension being the parish chapel):
The red carpets, the gilded mirrors,
The brass stair-rods, the swing-doors within swing-doors
Like veil upon veil of a temple
Proceeding to an inner sanctum, the plush
Tip-up seats, the hush when the lights dimmed,
The girl acolyte strapped to her tray
Of tubs of ice cream and beakers with straws,
Floor-to-ceiling wine-red curtains being parted
To reveal the forbidden silver screen, and he
Seated beside his mother in the public dark,
Safe in the abyss, gazing up
At the soft black rain of her hair,
Her mouth glistening with plum-red lipstick,
Her white pearl necklace, her white pearl earrings.
What could be more vista-rich for a six-year-old boy
Than to be seated in cinema darkness at his first film
With his young mother, his first sweetheart?
Larger-than-life pictures on the screen

Filled him with freedom, longing, dread:
When horses appeared on the crest of a hill,
Galloping cross-country to the port of Bristol,
He ducked his head in his seat for fear
Of being trampled to death by their onrushing hooves.
Long John Silver made a grand entrance
As the buccaneer to beat all buccaneers,
Parrot on shoulder,
With a glass of rum and a gleaming eye,
And his unshaven, bristling black chin
And his one leg and his West Country piratical voice
        and
A small boy on his sixth birthday gripped tight his
        mother's hand.
The first film of his life she had chosen
To bring him to was *Treasure Island*
Starring Robert Newton as Long John Silver,
Denis O'Dea as Dr Livesey
And Spike Milligan as Ben Gunn.
In his cinema seat he became Jim Hawkins
Sitting in secret at the bottom of the barrel,
Overhearing things a boy should never overhear.
For the first time he understood
That the price of knowledge is death.
When they emerged out of the film
As out of a book of the Old Testament,
Day had changed into night and it was raining;
All of Dublin was black water and city lights
And his mother queued for a Number 11 bus.
They sailed home aboard the *Hispaniola*
To the coal fire and the brass tongs,
By which they lolled until he fell asleep.
As surely as God created heaven and earth
Thenceforth, aged six years, his life,
In all its people and in all its places,

Would be a *Treasure Island*
A tropic idyll forever under threat,
A geography revealed to him by his mother,
Sweet Sheila MacBride, who had married John Durcan,
One of the black, red-roaring, fighting Durcans of
  Mayo.

Golden Mothers Driving West

The inevitable call came from the Alzheimer's nursing
    home.
Mummy had been sitting there in an armchair for two
    years
In a top-storey room with two other agèd ladies,
Deborah O'Donoghue and Maureen Timoney.
Three Irish orang-utans, silent, stationary.
The call was to say that between 3 and 5 a.m.
The three of them had gone missing from the room.
At first it was thought that all three had slipped
Out the window, ajar in the hot, humid night.
But, no, there were no torsos in the flowerbed.
It transpired that a car had also gone missing.
Was it thinkable they had commandeered a car?
At five in the afternoon the police called
To say that a Polish youth in a car wash in Kinnegad
Had washed and hot-waxed a car for three ladies,
All of whom were wearing golden dressing gowns –
Standard issue golden dressing gowns
Worn by all the inmates of the Alzheimer's nursing
    home.
Why he remembered them was that he was struck
By the fact that all three ladies were laughing
For the ten minutes it took him to wash the car.
'I am surprised,' he stated, 'by laughter.'
At 9 p.m. the car was sighted in Tarmonbarry
On the Roscommon side of the River Shannon,
Parked at the jetty of the Emerald Star marina.
At 9.30 p.m. a female German child was taken
To the police station at Longford by her stepfather.
The eleven-year-old had earlier told her stepfather
In the cabin of their hired six-berth river cruiser
That she had seen three ladies jump from the bridge.

Her stepfather had assumed his daughter imagined it
As she was, he told police, 'a day-dreamer born'.
The girl repeated her story to the police:
How three small, thin, agèd ladies with white hair
Had, all at once, together, jumped from the bridge,
Their dressing gowns flying behind them in the breeze.
What colours were the dressing gowns? she was asked.
'They are wearing gold,' she replied.
Wreathed on the weir downstream from the bridge
Police sub-aqua divers retrieved the three bodies,
One of whom, of course, was my own emaciated
        mother,
Whose fingerprints were later found on the wheel of
        the car.
She had been driving west, west to Westport,
Westport on the west coast of Ireland
In the County of Mayo,
Where she had grown up with her mother and sisters
In the War of Independence and the Civil War,
Driving west to Streamstown three miles outside
        Westport,
Where on afternoons in September in 1920,
Ignoring the roadblocks and the assassinations,
They used walk down Sunnyside by the sea's edge,
The curlews and the oystercatchers,
The upturned black currachs drying out on the stones,
And picnic on the machair grass above the seaweed,
Under the chestnut trees turning autumn gold
And the fuchsia bleeding like troupes of crimson-tutu'd
        ballerinas in the black hedgerows.
Standing over my mother's carcass in the morgue,
A sheep's skull on a slab,
A girl in her birth-gown blown across the sand,
I shut my eyes:
Thank you, O golden mother,

For giving me a life,
A spear of rain.
After a long life searching for a little boy who lives
    down the lane
You never found him, but you never gave up;
In your afterlife nightie
You are pirouetting expectantly for the last time.

Praise in Which I Live and Move and Have My Being (2012)

October Early Morning Haircut

In the barber shop early this morning in Baggot
    Street the barber
Turned out to be an Algerian Berber – a young
    man descended
From the original, indigenous peoples of Algeria
Who populated that immense territory long, long
    before
The Arabs and much later the French.
He was a tall, dark, curly-headed young man
Dressed all in black,
Quiet, not garrulous, reserved, reticent,
Concentrating on the job in hand,
My hoary, old, white head overgrown
Like my garden and everything else in my life.
He snipped and trimmed in meditative silence.
I mentioned a recent murder in the neighbourhood
(A so-called 'road-rage murder'
In which an Irish motorist had snatched a hurley
    stick from his car boot
And beat the brains out of the other driver – an
    Englishman).
One topic led to another,
Which of course is the beauty of conversation,
Its purpose and meaning, and next thing
The Algerian Berber barber was telling me
How only the other morning he'd been cutting the
    hair
Of an archaeology professor, and how this client
Had stated that it may have been the Berbers of
    Algeria
Who 6,000 years ago BC
Constructed Newgrange – the most famous
    monument in Ireland,

Fabled and fabulous, older than the pyramids,
A vast circular tumulus that to this day
Has always looked more like the creation
Of people from outer space.
'Yes,' responded my barber lugubriously but
        proudly,
'But you see, sir, the Berbers *are* from outer space.'
I stared into the long looking glass at his dark face
Wide-eyed over my white head,
Delicately twirling his scissors.
'Yes,' he repeated solemnly, almost inaudibly,
'My people – the Berbers of Algeria –
Are people from outer space.'
Nodding his head, he added:
'Are you a pensioner, sir?'
The first time in my life
Anyone had ever asked me that question.
'Well, as a matter of fact,
Yes, I am a pensioner!'
'In that case, sir,' he smiled eagerly, gently,
Showing me all of his snow-white white teeth,
'It will be six – not sixteen – euro.'
Out on the street for the rest of the morning
I had to keep restraining myself
From breaking out into frolics,
From playing hopscotch with myself.
What would the cultural police
Texting and emailing their victims –
Tweeting and twittering –
Have to say about a 66-year-old white-haired man
Playing hopscotch with himself on the streets of
        Dublin city?

ICI REPOSE VINCENT VAN GOGH
1853–1890

I

Gare du Nord, 9.56 AUVERS DIRECT:
Having the get-up-and-go to make the journey is
    what matters –
Copping on that it is a *day-trip*
As well as a *pèlerinage*
To the grave of a hero who took his own life
But who did not commit suicide;
The accidental company of two young women
In the same train carriage
Holding hands, kissing, gossiping
Ten to the dozen, ten to the dozen
The way young lovers do;
'Lesbians in their loveliness';
The automobile mechanic, six feet six of him,
With his tin box of watercolour paints, his sketch
    pads,
His fold-up stool, his rucksack of litres of water –
All day he'll sit at the grave impervious
To the bad manners of some, the courtesy of others;
The seventy-year-old Irishman in a green baseball
    cap,
A shamrock on its crest above its visor,
Around his neck
A Nikon camera weighing half a kilo;
Discreet but decisive in his picture-making.
On a scorching hot day of thirty degrees
Up on the plateau of golden wheat fields
Under the whirling, swooping crows
Where there is no shelter from the sun
A cry of a man rang out and a shot was heard:

I see in my members another law
At war with the law of my mind.

II

Back at the Gare du Nord on the 18.18 AUVERS DIRECT
The day trippers – even the young lovers –
Are too fatigued to speak – too fatigued almost to
      crawl
The tunnels of the metro, splitting up
To seek out the different lines with different termini,
Place d'Italie, Porte d'Orléans, Porte de Clignancourt.

In the Place de l'Estrapade in the 5th *arrondissement*
By a small, three-tiered, wrought-iron, green-painted
      fountain
With six spouts and a circular granite rim
In the shade of twelve paulownia trees,
Large, widespread, translucent emerald leaves,
Incarnations of their blue flowers over,
Long-legged trunks so lean, so spare,
Oriental trees,
Two day trippers to the ivy-duvet'd grave in Auvers-
      sur-Oise,
Where two brothers sleep back to back,
Their feet facing south,
Crouch on a wrought-iron, green-timbered bench in
      silence,
Watching children tightrope-walking on the rim
Of the fountain, two other vagrants with bottles of
      red wine
Having a quiet, tranquil, calm, intense dialogue,
Two Arab women in veils, mother and daughter
With seven-year-old son.

I close my eyes and listen to the fountain –
To those other voices Arab women know
And that light-starved man from the black north:
I see in my members another law
At war with the law of my mind.

Morning Ireland, Be Warned!

I was cast as the Angel Gabriel
In the school Christmas play.
Next day when my mother
Asked me to take off my wings
(The Kellehers were coming to lunch –
My wings would only get in the way of things)
I demurred and when she asked me again
I cried out to her, ' No, no, Mummy! No, no, no!
I am going to stay being the Angel Gabriel
For all of my life!'
        That was fifty-eight years ago
And this morning as I kneel alone in the chapel
Before the empty cradle in the Christmas crib
I can feel myself again rustling my wings,
Getting ready to announce the news again.
Morning Ireland, be warned!

Slievemore Cemetery Headstones

I

KATTIE CARR 1929–1995

She is my song, my turf-stack, my whitewashed wall.
She is my house in the hill up above me.
She is my young woman facing west.
She is my seashell I place to my ear.
She is my ocean I go to sleep and wake up to.

II

MICHAEL CARR 1929–2009

He is my man across the Irish Sea,
My hero of fidelity, who every Friday
Sends me home his wages to rear our family.
Stepping off the bus at the crossroads with his suitcase,
His cardboard boxes of dolls, a sailboat, a tricycle.
He is home now for good, beside me forever.

The Clothes Line

I'm sixty-four and do you know why it is
When there's a bit of sun I sit out
On a kitchen chair in the yard beside the clothes line?
The clothes on the clothes line
Keep me company:
A pair of white chinos leaping up and down
In a whirling breeze;
A blue bath towel wrapping itself around itself;
Two black T-shirts bragging their bare black chests;
Two pairs of black boxer shorts
Crinkling slightly, their careers almost over;
A red jumper hanging dead, as if playing dead;
Two pairs of black socks open-mouthed like four drunk
    bores;
Striped pyjama bottoms giving me the two fingers,
Their top facing down the black TV dish over my head,
Yet seeming to trumpet at me through each trunk-like
    arm: WATCH IT!

After sixty-four years of companionship and conviviality,
On a summer's day
These are my friends – the friends I have left –
My clothes on the clothes line –
And even if they are – so to speak – silent friends –
Their arms, their legs, their torsos
Keep me company for an hour or two
And they are charitable enough to overlook my mortality.

Sandymount Strand Keeping Going

to Seamus Heaney on his seventy-second birthday

In the miraculous hour of mid-morning
Walking the promenade of Sandymount Strand,
Gazing out at the sun in splendour on Dublin Bay

After a flock of geese had flown low across the water,
The incoming tide with two hours more to come,
Labradors, collies, spaniels barking in vain,

On the path between the roadway and the bay
Walking from the Esso station at the Martello Tower
South towards the Merrion Gates

Over the tarmacadam where no feet were
Except for the running feet of young middle-aged women
Seeking the fingertip of a newborn king

I met one walking, methodically in measure,
As if on eggshells on electric wires.
He came walking out of the sun high in the sky

So that all I could decipher was a silhouette with hat,
Yet with the unmistakeable posture of his farmer father,
And as I fixed upon the upturned face

That affectionate surprise with which we recognise
The beloved visage of a long-lost friend
I caught the sudden look of the living maestro

Whom I had known some thirty-five years ago
But had never met on these exotic shores.
'Rio!' I exclaimed and with me he joined

In rejoicing in and celebrating Dublin Bay.
We trod the pathway in a springtime patrol.
I said: 'Are you facing East?'

He replied: 'Yes, I am facing East.'
We looked together to our right
Southwards to the sun climbing towards noon.

He said: 'To me it is all right of ways,
It is all poems, centuries, meditations
To my spirit appeased but peregrine

Among my granddaughters with my wife,
My daughter, my sons and their wives.'
I said: 'I am thinking it has been

A strange way to have spent one's life,
Fifty or more years composing poems.'
He nodded his head, concelebrated with heart.

He said: 'What has it been all about but to . . .
Donner un sens plus pur aux mots de la tribu.
What we must do must be done

On our own. The main thing
Is to write for the joy of it.
The English language belongs to us.'

We knew where we had come from, the medieval
    kingdoms
Of the 1940s, the ballrooms where he obeyed his mother's
    pleas
'Be sure and dance with the girls who are not asked.'

The sun was at its zenith. In the glittering and sparkling
    bay
He left me with a kind of valediction,
Fading into the whiteout of the angelus bell of the Star of
    the Sea.

My courageous comrade, what good stamina you own!
On what distant shore will you leave your body?
Be it Lake Garda or Erie, it will be close to home.

Staring Out the Window Three Weeks after his Death

On the last day of his life as he lay comatose in the hospital
    bed
I saw that his soul was a hare which was poised
In the long grass of his body, ears pricked.
It sprang toward me and halted and I wondered if it
Could hear me breathing
Or if it could smell my own fear, which was,
Could he but have known it, greater than his
For plainly he was a just and playful man
And just and playful men are as brave as they are rare.
Then his cancer-eroded body appeared to shudder
As if a gust of wind blew through the long grass
And the hare of his soul made a U-turn
And began bounding away from me
Until it disappeared from sight into a dark wood
And I thought – that is the end of that,
I will not be seeing him again.
He died in front of me; no one else was in the room.
My eyes teemed with tears; I could not damp them down.
I stood up to walk around his bed
Only to catch sight again of the hare of his soul
Springing out of the wood into a beachy cove of sunlight
And I thought: Yes, that's how it is going to be from now on.
The hare of his soul always there, when I least expect it;
Popping up out of nowhere, sitting still.

Free Travel Pass

The woman behind the counter hands me my
    Free Travel Pass,
Disgust scrawled all over her face.
I smile at her. I can't help smiling at her.
I say to her: 'Thank you, ma'am.'
She snaps: 'Don't *ma'am* me.'
I say: 'Oh but I must!
Now I can go anywhere for free
In the Republic of Ireland
And it's all thanks to you!'
She sniffs: 'Don't thank *me*.'
I cry: 'O my good lady, don't say that!'
She crows: 'Don't *good lady* me.
If you've no more business here,
The exit door is over there.'
I tango out into the street and
Refraining from a hop, skip and jump
I slide into a pharmacy
For a bottle of Night Nurse.
The ambient temperature is minus two degrees.

Having received a lecture on the dangers of
    codeine,
Instead of my credit card
I hand the cocky young female pharmacist
My Free Travel Pass.
She also snaps at me:
'Sir, that's your Free Travel Pass.'
'Oh, so it is!' I cry. 'Forgive me!
I have only this very morning
Received my Free Travel Pass and
I am so – so hyper – is that the word?
How I'd love to tango with you!'
She glares a very, very PC glare.

I board the Red Line tram to the Point,
Riding the docklands of Dublin like Don
      Quixote
On a camel especially imported from Valladolid.
To any other passenger who will listen
I whisper as surreptitiously as I can,
Seriously surreptitiously:
'You know – I've just been – given – the Free
      Travel Pass!'
Making a slight attempt to brandish it in their
      faces.
I want to share with them my sense of
      Recognition,
Of Affirmation, of Participation –
After sixty-six years of teetering in an island
      called Ireland
On the dark edge of Europe
I am the recipient of a Free Travel Pass!
When, exhausted and furious,
I come to die, if nothing else I can say
'I lived to receive the Free Travel Pass!'
After disembarking at the Point, I trek across the
      East Link Toll Bridge,
Meeting, halfway across, a naked, aged jogger in
      his seventies,
Naked except for a pair of scanty red briefs
In the ambient temperature of minus two degrees.
'By Harry,' I cry to him, 'but you're a hardy
      man!'
He grins a flamboyantly toothless grin.

I needed badly that lesson in humility.
I needed to be taken down a notch or two.
I walk the rest of the way home along Pigeon
      House Road,

Patting my breast pocket, my Free Travel Pass.
It would be just like you, old boy, to go and
      lose it
On your first day at school.

The Days of Surprise (2015)

57 Dartmouth Square

I was three years of age in the full of my days,
Never again to be so fully myself.
I was my home, my home was my name –
57 Dartmouth Square.
All that I was, now and for ever,
Today, yesterday and tomorrow,
57 Dartmouth Square.
Sometimes I was called Paul
But mostly I was not a who or a what
But a where.

I was a place.
In the sixty-odd years that were to follow
(Which fortunately I had no foreknowledge of)
I would never again know such apotheosis
As the place that I was, 1947–48.
I answered to the name of Paul, to that fearful call –
'Paul! Paul!' –
But knowing that my real name,
My identity tag stitched in red thread
On white cotton on my grey socks,
Was 57 Dartmouth Square.
Heaven was a place – not a placeless heaven –
And I was that place –
57 Dartmouth Square.

57 Dartmouth Square
Was a Victorian terrace house
On the Grand Canal in Dublin
Between Charlemont Street Bridge and Leeson
    Street Bridge
Built for British Army officers
And their families in the late 1890s.

1947–48 there was myself and my mother,
My father gone away for a long time
To stand in County Mayo in the general election
On the Clann na Poblachta ticket. With the ticket
He'd come home at weekends, presenting me with
      the ticket
To play with – roll upon roll of election tickets.

1947–48 when I walked in and out of myself,
57 Dartmouth Square,
Holding hands with Mummy,
I was a three-storey, red-brick terraced house
With two flights of granite steps to a hall door
With a recessed porch
In which I never dallied, not even to play in.
I entered only the basement to come in and out of
      myself,
The same as the coalman humping
Sacks of coal and slack on his bent shoulders,
The same as the newspaper man,
All twenty-one stone of him,
His tar-black streaky hair drenched in hair oil,
His yellow lined face more ancient than parchment.

Holding hands with Mummy on winter mornings
We'd walk along the Square, its high black palings,
Under house-high sycamores and limes,
To the far side of it where the Grand Canal,
High up in its road, flowed
From Charlemont Street Bridge to Leeson Street
      Bridge.

We'd climb up wide steps, Mummy and I,
And stand on the towpath to watch the barge
Inside the lock gates rising up

Like Jesus in the Resurrection story
Until the barge achieved its glory and began to chug
Between the banks, its cargo under tarpaulin,
A man in a cloth cap at the tiller, smoking a
    cigarette,
A man's bicycle thrown down at his feet on the
    deck,
All handlebars, crossbar, raw naked leather saddle.

Much as I enjoyed being 57 Dartmouth Square,
My name, role and function as 57 Dartmouth
    Square,
One day I'd cease to be 57 Dartmouth Square,
Becoming instead the *Barge Man at the Tiller*
In a Cloth Cap, smoking a cigarette.
It was my fate to be a happy neurotic.
In the winter of 1947–48 holding Mummy's hand,
Knowing where I was, I'd reached already the
    Promised Land,
The remainder of my life I would spend
Waiting for the Three Wise Men to find me.

6 May 1954 Dr Roger Bannister broke the four-
    minute mile
At the Iffley Road Track in Oxford
And being a skinlessly searching nine-year-old
    boy-child
I wanted also to break the four-minute mile.
Four laps of Dartmouth Square on the footpath
Constituted approximately the magic mile.
I went into training, racing around the Square
With the boy next door, John Richardson,
Hurtling around its corners, tut-tutting pedestrians
Stepping aside to pre-empt catastrophic collisions.

The Square was padlocked and in winter
The girls of the Loreto Convent, St Stephen's Green,
Played hockey in it, a pre-Christian field game
From the era when a human being carried a club
        and a stone.
In my bedroom window I sat repining
And aching at their stickwork – flicking, pushing,
        scooping –
In their long tomato-red skirts, white shirts and ties.
Bully! Bully! Bully! Bully! Bully!
Pubescence is a beastly process.

In the summertime youths from The Hill on Mount
        Pleasant
Climbed over the high black palings to play soccer –
Only to be chased and beaten out of it by the
        Garda Síochána,
A respectable resident having telephoned a
        complaint:
A shocking epiphany of my child's accumulating
        horror
At the cracks – no, the chasms – in the social fabric
        of Dublin.

Christmas Day was not really Christmas Day,
It was the day of Santa Claus, an eccentric deity
Whom my father's corpulent pal, Judge Charlie
        Conroy,
Pointed out to me one night catwalking the
        rooftops.
The real Christmas Day was the Feast of the
        Epiphany, 6 January,
When at long and dear last in the suspenseful chess
        game of life
I got to move the Three Wise Men into the Crib.

At last they had found me and I wriggled in ecstasy.
How ecstatic also seemed these three exotic
        refugees,
Melchior, Caspar and Balthasar.
Hailing from the farthest corners of the universe,
From China, Lithuania, Ethiopia.
On the Feast of the Epiphany
In the hallway of 57 Dartmouth Square
Into the Crib on the hall table
I moved the Three Wise Men into position,
A stick of liquorice dangling from my mouth.
I had become again the happy neurotic I aspired
        to be.

First Mixed Party

In 1959, aged fifteen, I was invited to a mixed party –
A MIXED party! –
In the house of Mr and Mrs Thomas Doyle, S.C.
In Winton Road off the Appian Way
By printed invitation,
Black italics on gilt-edged white card.
After a council of war my parents gave me permission,
My father ruling against it, but my mother overruling
       him;
The MIXTURE being surprisingly of boys and girls,
Caterpillars and tigers, corncrakes and polar bears.
Up till then I had only ever been at orgies for little boys
At which we beat each other up with pillows and
       cushions,
Doing our damnedest to wreck our parents' homes.

To the gramophone accompaniment of Buddy Holly
       super-stuttering
'Peggy Sue' and 'Rave On',
Elvis Presley – 'incarnate evil' our Jesuit maths teacher
       had confided in us –
Honking huskily on a leash 'Hound Dog'
Or shivering catatonically in his 'Blue Suede Shoes'
Or oiling his adenoids with 'Wooden Heart',
Jerry Lee Lewis going off his rocker,
Boys and girls circled around each other,
Animals not of different species but from different
       planets.
I gawked at clusters of teenage females
As if they were flocks of ostriches
Which they were – except
For the two or three orang-outangs among them
Whom we pimply puritanical prigs

Knowingly dismissed as 'flirts' –
Not knowing what the word 'flirt' meant – exactly.

I, of course, immediately fell in love with Fiona,
Being a lifelong mortally wounded Romantic
Since the age of four and a half.
I had my first love affair at seven
With Andrea who had freckles and red hair –
She walked to school on the other side of the road,
Eyed by me already in the viral clutches of Venus;
I dumped her for Jacqueline, who also had freckles and
    red hair,
Because Jacqueline sat on the grass with me making
    daisy chains.

After three hours of agonised eyeballing
And the central light had been switched off
Leaving only one standard lamp and two table lamps,
When we thought nobody was looking
We exchanged telephone numbers, Fiona and I.
The next day when I came home from school
In the blackening gloom of a late North European
    afternoon,
My mother in the cold dark kitchen to which she had
    been consigned in perpetuity,
Sighing, stammered: 'Your father wants to speak to you
    in The Study.'

My father had a room of his own
Which he called The Study.
He stood up from behind his desk
And grimaced at me with incredulity:
'Do you know what you have done?'
Quivering – I knew where this dialogue was going to
    conclude –

I replied truthfully 'No'.
He continued – waving his right arm in the air
Like Robespierre addressing the Estates-General
(My father was a devotee of Robespierre) –
'Do you know from whom I have received a
      telephone call?'
'N – n – no' I replied, barely able to stutter.
'Mrs Mona O'Connor – one of the most respectable
Ladies in the whole of the island of Ireland –
Mrs Mona O'Connor of Roscommon.
Do you know what she told me?
Mrs Mona O'Connor of Roscommon informed me
That at that social whatever-it-was last night,
Which in the first place you never should have
      attended,
You were observed – observed! – wearing a – a – a –
      a BLACK shirt!'
Whereupon instead of unbuckling his trousers belt
With which to give me an unmerciful thrashing,
Which would be his normal course of action,
He slumped back down into his swivel chair, groaning:
'A black shirt!
Are you cognisant of what you have done?
A black shirt!
Where did you come from? Who are you?
Will I always have to be ashamed of you for the rest
      of my days?
Mrs Mona O'Connor of Roscommon, *what* will she
think of us?'

Ash Wednesday, Dublin,
13 February 2013

'I see you've got your ashes!'
'My what?'
'You've got your ashes on your forehead!'
'Oh, yes, I have.'
The cute old man in my local supermarket –
A small, gay Dublin man with a silver Chaplin
    moustache.
The first time in twenty-five years
He has spoken to me and he is not finished:
'Are you looking forward to the conclave?'
'The what?'
'The conclave – you know – for the new Pope.'
(Two days ago, the German Shepherd had
    resigned.)
'Yes, I am – it will be a key conclave.'
'Do you know what I am hoping?' –
He leans over the counter, all confidential –
'I'm hoping it'll be a black fellow.
We're in dire need of a black fellow.
We've had enough of all those white fellows –
Two thousand years of white fellows.
It's high time for a black fellow.
Don't you agree, sir?'
He beams at me with the happy prospect.

In the doorway I peer out at a vista
Of black popes, lines of them,
In the drizzling rain,
Far as the eye can see.
Alleluia!
The hegemony of the white man is over.
If not in sackcloth but in ashes,

I will pray not only for a black pope
But for a black Archbishop of Dublin.
We Irish also have had enough
Of the hegemony of the white Irishman.
What is more, I will pray like a madman
For a black woman Archbishop of Dublin.
I am dust, and unto dust I shall return.

The Days of Surprise

The morning after the election of Francis,
In Ringsend Church at 11.45 a.m.,
Empty except for the smudge of my own presence –
Serious silence. *Silenzio!*
The sole sound is the sound of silence:
Silenzio, which is the chord of the lowly, chosen one,
Jorge Mario Bergoglio of Buenos Aires,
Silenzio, which is the carnival of his soul,
Silenzio, which is the mother and father of effortlessness,
Silenzio, which is the concentration of the child,
Silenzio, which is singing
'I am listening to you';
Silenzio, which is whispering 'Let me embrace you';
Silenzio, which is smiling 'Let me kiss your feet.'

At the altar-rail I gaze
At the noticeboard of the First Holy Communion children,
Each with their unique pledge:
Rosita Mulhall, aged 7:
'I PROMISE TO CLEAN MY ROOM.'
Chloe Swift, aged 8:
'I PROMISE TO PLAY WITH LUKE.'
Lisa Jordan, aged 7:
'I PROMISE TO FOLLOW JESUS
BY HOOVERING FOR MY MAM.'

Outside, around the church, the village swirls
And swarms like the hundreds of brent geese
Jinking overhead and the seagulls swooping
Like in a painting by a child or Mark Joyce
Or Gerard Dillon or Giotto or Fra Angelico
Or Ian Fairweather or Nicolas de Staël or Tony O'Malley.
As the church bell tolls the angelus at noon

The traffic lights conduct the people,
The buildings in the village like in Buenos Aires
All at angles with one another –
All gables, chimney pots, railings –
The barber shop, Tesco Express, HQ Dry Cleaners,
The three public houses – The Yacht, The Oarsman,
        Sally's Return –
The Bridge Café, the pharmacy, Ladbrokes bookmaker's,
The library with its Chinese granite benches,
The health centre, the Master Butcher's,
Ferrari's Takeaway, Spar,
The charity shop, the wine shop, the humpbacked bridge
Under which, behind Ringsend Church, the River
        Dodder flows
Like a little mare over the last fence
At Cheltenham or Punchestown,
Before it breasts the line at the winning post,
Its rider bent over double
Like the Angel at the Annunciation,
And meets the River Liffey and the sea.

The tide is in and Francis has come back
From Assisi to stroll again amongst us,
To announce the affinity of all creatures –
Child, kitten, woman, puppy, man, lamb, foal,
Prisoner, judge, sick, elderly,
Buggy baby, Zimmer-frame lady.
On the ledge between the church gable and the high river,
Alongside the council flats of the working people –
The aristocracy of the poor –
The flood-lit, blue-and-white statue on its Dublin
        granite plinth –
Our Lady, barefoot, smiling upon the waters,
And upon Jorge Mario Bergoglio – Papa Francesco.

Standing up in the back of an open jeep
In the middle of the piazza in his white shop coat,
Instead of the Papal Blessing
He gives us the thumbs-up sign –
'Have a nice Sunday, have a good lunch';
Smiling a good smile,
Again he gives us the thumbs-up sign –
'This is what we do in Argentina –
Be amicable to your neuroses.'

From the hump of the bridge I say to him,
With the greyhound track behind me
And the Sugar Loaf and the Dublin mountains,
Brimming with *silenzio*, Thomas Merton's prayer:
'May the Most Holy Mother of God
Obtain for your soul light and peace and strength
And may her Holy Child
Be your joy and protection at all times.'

14 March 2013

The Young Mother on the Country Bus in El Salvador

On a country bus in El Salvador
About twenty-eight years ago,
Father Sam found himself seated next
A young Salvadoran mother
Breastfeeding her infant daughter.
Father Sam blurted out:
'*Que hermosa niña!*
What a beautiful baby girl!'
She smiled and when she came
To the end of a passage of breastfeeding
She took Father Sam's right hand
In her own right hand
And placed it across her left breast:
'It is good, Papa,' she smiled, 'it is good.'

The Azores High

The women who present the weather forecast on
    Irish TV –
Jean Byrne, Evelyn Cusack, Siobhán Ryan, Nuala
    Carey –
Are the modern-day successors
To the music-hall cabaret singers of the late nineteenth
    century,
Whom we see in the paintings of Manet, Sickert,
    Degas:
The top echelon in Paris and London.
The doyenne of them all is without question Jean
    Byrne,
Although Siobhán Ryan in short-sleeve scarlet frock
Gives Jean Byrne a close run for starry mystique –
Her deep-sea, coming-up-for-air disclosures –
Her swivelling-in-profile-to-camera closing-shot
    technique –
Her pigtail drooling down one bare left shoulder.
Men as well as women race home from work to catch
Jean Byrne's weather forecast at the end of the Six
    One News.
What a luxury it is to lie back on your own sofa
After a long, mindless day's work as Secretary General
Of the Department of Going Forward or Acting Head
    of Going Backwards,
Kick off your slip-on, official black shoes
And watch Jean Byrne perform her latest forecast –
Revealing to you – and you alone – the state of the
    cosmos,
Its innermost secrets, its most intimate details:
'There's a cold front approaching from the east . . .
Yet at the same time approaching from the west
There is an associated suggestion of an Azores High

North-west of Madeira and Porto Santo
Over Newfoundland and Labrador
That might – just might – be coming our way . . .
Reading 10 to 15 hectopascals . . .
But – let's look now at our rainfall predictive
            sequence . . .
A pretty even distribution of showers for this
            evening . . .'
Last night in her body-hugging, all-black, belted silk
            dress
Slit with a sash of lavender-pink,
Her chunky silver necklace and bracelets,
Her block-glass earrings,
She turned her back on you to scan her chart.
Noel, one of our security men – a roly-poly little man
Staring out the porter's office window – sighs:
'They say she's got a huge male following.'

This evening you gaze up at her on the thirty-two-inch
            plasma
Over the fireplace –
Black, sleeveless, zipper-pocketed, denim shirt
Studded with pearl-white buttons
Over bottle-green, skin-tight denim jeans –
A Waterford glass bracelet on her left wrist –
As, caressing her zapper – *her* remote –
She turns around or half-around,
Keeping one eye on her audience – *you* –
And one eye on her weather chart behind her.
When she hits a high note with 'cold front'
In her school-girl contralto
It's like a pillow for your mind!
She bats her eyelashes and she splashes you
With mascara and eyeliner

And her scarlet lipstick smearing your white shirt
    collar,
Like your late mother's homemade raspberry jam,
Until at the climax of her meteorological chanson
She looks you straight in the eye, daggers,
Four-square, and, pausing her pause, she whispers:
'Tonight will be another damp and humid night –
Tomorrow another hot day, but a little hazier in the
    north-west –
With somewhat even hotter conditions during the
    weekend:
I'll leave you with your summary chart, goodnight,
    take care.'

The Killing of Marie Colvin

(d. 22 February 2012)

I

1959 in a tiny public park in New York on a sunny
    morning
A big bald guy in a tracksuit, hands on hips,
His two-and-three-quarters-year-old daughter scooting
    around him.
Already she has mastered the art of the scooter with
    authority.
Two and three-quarters and she cannot put a foot wrong
In her pink-and-orange windcheater, blue jeans, white
    plimsolls,
Her fair hair flying behind her, blue eyes gleaming,
And when she has done she does not throw down her
    scooter –
She parks it at the kerb and puts her hands over her eyes
To try and discern the shape and substance of her father.

II

2012 in a cocktail bar in Beirut, Lebanon,
Two middle-aged women perch on high stools at the bar,
Weighing up the pros and cons of taking up the offer
To cross over into Syria by a smuggler's route,
Bringing them into the heart of the massacre in the city
    of Homs.
Lindsey Hilsum, than whom there is no war reporter
    more honest
Or courageous or wise – weighing it all up –
Considers that the risk is too great, that even the
    great duty
Of reporting the massacre of civilians in Homs

Cannot justify going to what looks like one's own
    certain death.

Marie Colvin mutters, 'You're goddamn right, Lindsey,'
Swirls the swizzle stick in her rum and coke,
Adjusts the yellow curls on the nape of her neck,
Inserts her little finger into the band of her black
    eyepatch,
Grins at her cherished friend, sighs 'I'm off –
See you next week on these same two stools, all right?'

III

Seven days later in a firestorm of government shelling,
By command of His Excellency, President Bashar al-Assad,
In the Baba Amr quarter of the city of Homs in Syria,
Marie Colvin, aged fifty-six, lies mortally wounded,
Spilling her blood and guts alongside a headless child,
Her last heard words, her last known words:
'Why have we been abandoned by the world?'
Her shoes in the hallway alone surviving her killers.
Back in Beirut in an impasse high on a cliff, Lindsey
    Hilsum
Tries to keep walking on, her angered-out eyes placating
    no one.

The Man of Advancing Years and the Girl on a Bicycle

A man of advancing years, about ten years younger
    than myself,
Is turning right at the lights in his two-door,
    metallic-silver Ford Fiesta –
'Making a right', as they drawl stateside –
From Grand Canal Street into Clanwilliam Place,
While a cyclist is taking her time on her pedals
    pedantically,
Being young, carefree, nonchalant, emitting femininity.
In frustration, at first he brandishes his right arm
But concurrently, in a tantrum, he clenches his veiny,
    mottled fist,
Glaring over at me at my wheel for male moral support:
'No siree!' – I smile – 'No siree!
Did you not learn at your potted, privileged, exclusive,
Fee-paying, Holy Ghost boarding school long ago
That the girl on a bicycle always takes precedence?
Always the not-yet pregnant Mother of God?'

The Twenty-Four-Hour Piano Recital

'Where are you going?' she asked me.
I replied: 'I am walking you to your car.'
Seeming almost to mutter, she remonstrated: 'No need
    for that!'
She – a woman of particular manners, particular affections;
A woman of a lifetime of hard work and undiluted
    leisure.
When we got to her car, I opened the driver's door:
She glanced up at me, almost glaring at me:
'I am not used to men opening doors for me.'
She climbed in, putting her head down to insert the
    ignition key
And, surplus to requirements, I crawled away.
Above me a clutch of pine trees was shaking its head
And around the corner in the doorway of a boutique,
Opposite a boarded-up grocery store,
A lone, bare-headed gentleman
Was xylophoning tears from his eyes,
Pretending otherwise.
A Vale of Tears in the Suburbs of Dublin –
In which there is no escaping
Young, bow-tied Death waiting for all of us around
    the corner,
Sitting upright at his black piano, taking his time,
Sitting upright all day at his black piano,
Sitting upright all night at his black piano,
Turning sideways to smile at us from time to time,
Serenading you 'I'll meet you in Venice at
    Christmas-tide!'
As I drive up and down the switchback suburban hills
Back to my own palazzo of loneliness in the city –
A tearful, crumpled-up, little kip of a shoebox

Behind 'The Ruari Quinns' – the new council housing
      estate,
Named after a petite, goatee-bearded, local politician,
Down the docklands, the River Liffey willing itself out
      into Dublin Bay.
I'll tell you what it is and what it is not:
In the Twenty-Four-Hour Piano Recital in our sixties
I am a dependent man and she is an independent
      woman –
One of the First Realists, one of the Last Romantics.

Breaking News

I was driving up the mountain
Through the fuchsia and the sheep –
Horned black faces –
At 11.30 a.m. in the morning
Of the last Friday in August
When, fingers slipping on the dials,
Clambering out to unbolt the six-barred gate,
I switched on the radio accidentally:
'The death has been announced of the poet Seamus
        Heaney.'
A mist loomed, cloaking each sheep, sheep by sheep,
Shrouding all of the mountain and the western sea.

Inside the house the first chill of autumn.
I block-built a few firelighters in the grate,
Kindling, peat briquettes,
Struck a FIRESIDE safety match, white flames leaping up,
And down the chimney rustled Seamus's antiphonal
Derry brogue (undiluted by Harvard, Berkeley, Oxford,
        the BBC, Carysfort, RTÉ, Queen's)
'Are you all right down there, Poet Durcan?'
(That's how he always addressed me down thirty-seven
        years –
'Poet Durcan')
'Calm down, I'm only dead, I'm only beginning
The new life, only hours and minutes into it;
I miss my wife, my children, my grandchildren, my
        brothers,
Most of all my mighty spouse – otherwise
I've become the spaceman I've always longed to be –
In flight – breaking the sound barrier out in the
        cosmos –

Which, since boyhood – the American Air Force in our
     fields –
The aerodromes between our hedgerows –
Has always been my dream, my home, my Elysium –
After a lifetime of being neither here nor there –
Of being Kidnapped by Time –
I am out in the cosmos –
Tramping the Milky Way with my father and mother –
Our neighbour Rosie Keenan singing shut-eyed at the
     well –
Tiepolo skies salmon-pink, white, gold beneath our
     feet –
Never getting above ourselves, what it's all about –
Damascus, Athens, Jerusalem, children –
Down there below us, north-west Europe –
Anahorish, Mossbawn, Bellaghy –
Swarms of midges in veiled autumn evening light –
Anna Rose, Aibhín, Síofra – the other world –
And now I put the key for the first time
Into the door of my father's house.'

30 August 2013

Wild, Wild Erie (2016)

Lady Bartender at Home with a Souvenir Dog, New Orleans, La., 1964

after Diane Arbus

Honey I'm not kidding you!
With my charcoal eye-liner I'm not in my first youth –
Lonesome Lady Bartender at Home am I tonight –
A Manicured Poodle on a trolley is all well and good but . . .
What I need, what I demand, what I am going to devour
Are my old man's two German Shepherd Alsatian dogs
And then I'll be smiling-snarling like a tom-cat lording it over you!
My High German Roped-up Bleached Poodle Hair-Do!
My 50-dollar nylon plait, my turtleneck,
My leopard-skin waistcoat, my leather boots,
My Jack of Hearts in Wrought-Iron – Bilateral Symmetry –
Cute, isn't it? SAY it's cute – 33 times after me!
I'm 33.
Honey I'm not kidding you!
And then I'll be smiling-snarling like a tom-cat lording it over you!